Amy Nickell is a journalist and whether she is oversharing in newspapers and magazines, such as the *Metro*, the *Guardian* and *Grazia*, or in front of the camera offering Jennifer Aniston Doritos, she's never taken a standard approach. But the real surprise came when Amy discovered she was pregnant and without a boyfriend. Despite the bad press, unplanned pregnancy and single parenthood didn't ruin her life and she's been writing and talking about it ever since including appearances on *Good Morning Britain* and BBC Radio 4's *Woman's Hour*. She now lives in Berkhamsted, Hertfordshire with her son Freddy who is now three. Her favourite Spice Girl is Geri and she eats one avocado every day.

PRAISE FOR *CONFESSIONS OF A SINGLE MUM*

'This goes off like a rocket and never lets up . . . this
is like going out with your best mate for a coffee
and them telling you their whole experience'
Penny Smith

'Amy's frank and down-to-earth story is inspiring and honest'
*The Sun*

'What a great read.' ★★★★★
Matt Coyne, Man Vs. baby

WHAT AMAZON READERS
ARE SAYING ABOUT THE BOOK

'You don't have to be a single mum or female to love
this book! Amy is an absolute hero and role model to
everyone. Unbelievably funny and inspirational!'

'Hilarious and heartwarming'

'A refreshing insight into life as a single mum.
Had me laughing from page one!'

'It had me feeling all of the feels throughout and
is the fastest I have got through a book in ages as
I didn't want to put it down'

'By far the most entertaining book I've read this year – a
refreshing, feel-good, hilarious and touching must-read'

# CONFESSIONS OF A Single MUM

## AMY NICKELL

H

**HEADLINE**

First published in 2018
by HEADLINE PUBLISHING GROUP

First published in paperback in 2019

1

Cataloguing in Publication Data is available from the British Library

Paperback ISBN 978 1 4722 5790 1

Typeset in Chaparral by CC Book Production

Printed and bound in Great Britain by
Clays Ltd, Elcograf S.p.A.

HEADLINE PUBLISHING GROUP
An Hachette UK Company
Carmelite House
50 Victoria Embankment
London
EC4Y 0DZ

www.headline.co.uk
www.hachette.co.uk

For my brother, Martin

# CONTENTS

Introduction   ix

A Letter to Freddy   xiii

1. Big Boobs, Bigger Problem   1

2. Knocked up Without the Hollywood Ending   17

3. What Goes in, Must Come out   35

4. RIP Vagina   57

5. Falling in All the Love   75

6. Single Mum Myths Busted   93

7. Mummy, I Shrunk Your Tits   117

8. Mama's Got Bills to Pay   139

9. Getting Back on the Horse   161

10. You Can't Sit with Us   183

11. This Mum CAN Juggle   203

12. Where's MY Daddy?   225

Epilogue: Let's Get Real – Final Word   243

Ten Lessons Single Motherhood Has Taught Me   245

Further Resources   249

Acknowledgements   253

# INTRODUCTION

**W**ell, when is life really going to plan?

Hello! I'm Amy and, like you probably do, I had an idea of where I wanted my life to go. A life running order, you might say. Sort of like a set list a band might have. And by the time I'd got to twenty-three, it seemed to all be going to plan – things were very much on track. I had a good job, an all right (ish) boyfriend, good friends and I was a responsible pet owner to my frog Snoop, Frog. The train of life was chugging along its track completely to schedule. However, as with so many trains, there was signal failure ahead.

You know the standard life plan, right? I bet you have one just like it. It goes something like this . . . pass your exams, go to university, get a 2.1, get a good – preferably dream – job, find soulmate, get married to soulmate, make baby with soulmate, repeat within your financial means, live happily ever after, end life on the property ladder. Ta da, life plan COMPLETE. Certificate of excellence waiting for you at the pearly gates.

However, my life didn't end up sticking to the life order. Dunce hat for me. Instead – going back to my trusty band analogy – after the first few songs, my guitarist went on a rampage and ripped up the set list before smashing his own guitar over his head and admitting himself to the Priory.

When I was at university, I used to say that I wanted to be like Holly Willoughby who was married and had two children by the time she was thirty. Thirty years old, married to a TV producer and presenting *This Morning* – that was a bit of me, right there. My entry into motherhood, however, wasn't exactly the mirror image of Holly that I had hoped for. Ask little girls what they want to be when they grow up and I doubt any will say 'a single mum'. It's just not something we tend to want, is it? It's just something people off *Jeremy Kyle* do. I had an actual degree – I was clever, right? Surely my ovaries wouldn't betray me like that. When I was younger I thought girls who got pregnant unexpectedly must be pretty dim and if that did ever happen then the answer would be obvious. Then it did happen and guess what? The answer really wasn't obvious. Oh, and my baby's dad decided to bow out before the final act. Holly's nice producer husband never did that.

Cut forward nine months and I'm back in my hometown living with my parents in my mum's converted walk-in wardrobe with a brand-new addition – a little baby, Freddy. Now, no one saw that coming. Especially my mother who thought she'd raised me better than to make an error like that.

But then something really incredible happened. My unplanned baby didn't ruin my life. Rather, he made it. He taught me love I never knew possible, happiness I'd only seen hinted at before. And everything turned out more than OK; it turned out better than I ever could have imagined. My new life trumped my old life and I became a family. A family of two.

I just wish someone could have told me this when I weed on that stick and all I could see lying ahead was doom, gloom, dark circles and stretch marks. I was terrified and I really needn't have been.

So please, for the sake of future girls like me, can we stop judging for just a second. We might not be being carted off to mother and baby homes any more but the stigma is still very real. I know because I am judged every day. But being a parent isn't about your marital status. You can be happy, fabulous and dare I say, flourish as a mum or a dad whether you've never married, you're about to get hitched for the fifth time or you are three times divorced.

But getting here was an epic rollercoaster and it has taken me a long time to own my single mum status. I hope my story can inspire people to realise that there isn't a ranking system or a 'best' type of family. It's so engrained in our societal psyche that we have to keep things traditional like Holly Willoughby in order to be happy. Nuclear families are still the archetype for happiness.

This book is for the one in three – the odd Instamum out. There are loads of us but we don't have a voice and we've got a LOT to say. I wrote this for anyone who's apologised on a date that they are a mum. For anyone who thinks they need to download a dating app like Plenty of Fish to make their family a 'unit'. For all the women who send me messages on Facebook saying they never felt proud as parents just because they ended up, through no fault of their own, doing it solo. For any single mum boss who is not only owning but loving her solo parenting journey as much I am.

Families come in all shapes and sizes; it's the capacity to love that's important. If you can do that, you will be an amazing parent whatever your circumstances. Single parents don't need your pity, we just need your support. I want to make life just a little bit less petrifying for anyone who ever does find themselves doing something they always were told they shouldn't.

I snuck into motherhood uninvited. Arriving at motherhood was like I'd got on the wrong life train altogether and ended up in Leighton Buzzard. But when you do end up here, you realise life can be just fabulous. So if things haven't gone to plan then don't worry – this detour could be the best thing that ever happened to you.

The only plan I now have is to 'be happy' and if my family is that, then I know things ARE going to plan. There are countless possible futures and each one can be as happy and successful as the last. So hang in there, it's all going to be great. Whether you've just arrived, are on your way or been here a while, this is for anyone who's found themselves scratching their head and wondering, 'How the fuck did I end up here?'

# A LETTER TO FREDDY

My Freddy,

My little, my teeny weeny, my tiny, my pigsy; you are my piggles, my wiggles, my childish Bambino and my little gorgie man. These nicknames, I am sure, will serve you well into adulthood, and I'll be sad if at least one doesn't make it on to the back of a stag party T-shirt.

Today is your third birthday and as I write this you are tucked up in your bed, not mine for a change, having insisted that a box of six eggs lays next to your pillow (eggs are an inexplicable ongoing obsession of yours), while I tap away plagiarising your childhood on the laptop in the next room.

Three years ago today, on the day the iPhone 6 came out, as Goddy always reminds you, you gatecrashed into the world at 10.01 a.m. and everything I expected (I won't go into detail but it wasn't great stuff, no offence to the living you of now) – well, it just never came true.

Instead, you bring me a type of happiness I never even knew existed or was possible. You send my emotions through the wringer but you've helped me become me. I know I'm supposed to be nurturing and growing you (and I am, I promise – see potty training for more information) but you have changed ME in ways I had previously signed off and made redundant.

Four years ago I resigned myself to never feeling totally happy or confident. You changed all that. Somehow, call it biology, nature or just the fact you are the best, you made me feel both those things. You made me feel complete.

It's only now that I know you were planned all along. You were and still are the most perfect surprise that I never even knew I wanted. Without you, my life would be very boring, and I would still be coasting along, missing a part I didn't know I needed.

To summarise, you make my heart explode. No one can love anything as much as I love you. Maybe by the time you are able to read this, they'll have an invention that can measure and prove this. Either that or you'll just have to take my word and my daily barrage of cuddles as evidence.

Thank you for being such a bloody superstar. It's us against the world and I wouldn't have it any other way.

Lots of love,

Mummy

P.S. Sorry for sneaking in your room every single night and whispering these sentiments in your ear. I just never want you to underestimate just how much you are loved. That's why we don't need a dad – we've enough of everything just the way things are.

# 1

# BIG BOOBS, BIGGER PROBLEM

Finding out I was pregnant when I did . . . it came as a bit of a shock. I think I would have been less shocked to have woken up with gangrene. Or on the flip side, Harry Styles. Want to hear how it happened? Well, like all good stories, it starts off with a quadrupling in tit size.

'Your boobs are HUGE,' my friend said to me, grabbing one of my definitely larger-than-usual breasts. My flatmate, Lorcan, and I were holding our annual Simulation Christmas party for all our friends – basically, Christmas in January. We'd originally been so busy (well, drunk and disorganised) in December that we hadn't had time to have a Christmas party, so we decided to host our Simulation Christmas on 25 January. Think full-on Christmas tree, decorations, mulled wine, Noddy Holder – the works. We even had Secret Santa. Just a month late when, actually, everyone was very much over Christmas and looking forward to Spring.

Lorcan and I had been living together for two years, and he was, and is, my best friend in the world. 'Partners in crime' I think people would say about us, probably with an annoying wink, which fundamentally means we did loads of stupid stuff together, got really drunk and basically just had a right laugh. We still do, to be honest. We met while reading the news together on Leeds Student Radio four years earlier, both having individually decided that, obviously, that was our extra-curricular activity of choice. Damn Freshers' Fair. Based on this alone, it was always going to be a meeting of minds. After graduating we moved in together and were living in Golders Green in a rather lovely two-bed flat – all exposed brick and 'hygge' before it was even a thing. Just us two, our Harry Styles cardboard cutout and Snoop Frog, later joined by Blue Ivy the hamster, a rather unwise hungover impulse buy from the local pet shop. We thought Blue Ivy was a female, hence the name, until she inexplicably sprouted a pair of testicles about one month later.

At the time, Lorcan was working in PR and I was a celebrity reporter – we pretty much thought we were Edina and Patsy, and every Friday we would drink Prosecco (way before everyone else did) and shout 'We have it all!' out the window. We called it 'We Have It All Fridays'. Sort of like Meat-Free Mondays, but not as health conscious or involving Paul McCartney. We'd shout 'We have it all!' until one of the neighbours told us to shut up and then we would head off to Freedom in Soho for the next two nights and spend all day Sunday battling the fear and eating pizza. Sometimes we'd put on Liverpudlian accents and prank call our exes or boys whose numbers we'd got the night before. I really loved this period and still think it was the best fun I'll ever have. We always say we want '22', the age we

2

were then, tattooed on us somewhere because it really was a great time. Plus, I used to lie and say I was twenty-two until I was twenty-four. Basically, I spent two years after university being twenty-two, drinking Prosecco, interviewing Harry Styles and just having the biggest laugh. Sometimes all four at once, in fact. We made twenty-two cool WAY before Taylor Swift bothered.

Working as a celebrity reporter was the type of thing that my childhood dreams were stuffed with. A typical Monday for me around this time would involve going down to the *X Factor* studios to interview whoever had left the show the previous week. Then I would head to some brand's press day to blag as much free stuff as possible, before moving on to a 'PR lunch', where I would meet with a PR for a company that collaborates with pop stars and actors, supposedly to talk about potential media coverage I could give their clients, but actually I would just get free lunch and we would talk about who's having sex with who in their office – before moving on to who is secretly having sex with who in celebrity land. Then in the evening, I would be packed off to a red carpet event with my video producer Phil to, well, basically cause a breach of the peace. Our finest moment was perhaps turning up at the *Star Trek Into Darkness* premiere with me dressed as Princess Leia. Princess Leia from *Star Wars*, that is. For those unfamiliar, it was akin to wearing a devil onesie to church. Another time we charged the red carpet at the *Fast and Furious* premiere with me dressed as a policewoman to give Vin Diesel a speeding ticket. He called me the 'sexy side of the law' and it was all very thrilling slash excellent and forever etched in the 'proudest achievements' section of my brain. Things were very unserious. Things were a right bloody laugh.

So there we were hosting Simulation Christmas when I noticed I was getting very drunk much faster than usual, but I was quick to put this down to not having eaten that much. In fact, I hadn't eaten anything at all, because for the past week I'd been fairly certain that I'd had a touch of food poisoning as I had been feeling slightly peaky. Perhaps I was coming down with a cold? Or maybe I was iron deficient and almost definitely needed to get healthy and eat more broccoli?

In any case, despite the ACTUAL CHRISTMAS TREE, expertly sourced from a shop in Gloucestershire that genuinely sells Christmas decorations 365 days a year, fully decorated with a fairy on top – or more accurately a Geri Halliwell Spice Girls doll – it was something else that was getting all the attention.

'Your BOOBS!'

'WHERE HAVE THEY COME FROM?!'

'Have you just got a really good bra on?'

'You haven't had a free boob job, have you? I saw that press release!'

Pretty much every single human in attendance at that party had a comment to make about my chest. It hadn't had so much attention since the chicken fillet craze of '06. I made a careful mental note to wear this bra more often and then yawned yet again, wondering why I was so tired – it could only have been the stress of finding somewhere that stocks Christmas decorations in January. Genuinely very stressful.

'Hey – maybe you're PREGNANT. HAR HAR HAR,' my friend Charlotte joked as if that was just about the most hilarious thing possible. I concluded I must have gained weight which for once hadn't just gone straight to my bottom, and made a careful note to self to eat less Super Noodles and more vegetables. The party was a hit, despite no one eating the turkey and cranberry sauce sandwich platter I'd made. We played Justin Bieber's sorely underrated Christmas album and drank way too many weird liquors that I concluded belonged only in chocolates. By the end, I'd drunk so much cherry brandy that I felt very sick indeed.

The next morning, I have never felt so hungover. In all of my then twenty-four years, I had never been a throwing-up kind of drunk; in fact I always pitied that type as I have a huge, huge aversion to being sick. Like, I'm pretty sure I could be on a *This Morning* phobia segment about it. But that morning, there I was making friends with the toilet bowl and cursing the fact that I couldn't handle the festive cheer as well as I used to. I decided that I must be getting old: no longer could a bottle of Lucozade and twenty chicken nuggets cure a hangover, apparently. But then I realised my period hadn't come . . .

Being scatty since birth, I figured I had simply lost track of the date or was just a bit late that month. This knicker no-show was sure to turn up – I even had period pains as evidence. You don't get period pains if you are pregnant, do you? (N.B. Implantation pains. Very much a thing.) I mentioned my lack of period to my mum, who had come over to take me for lunch the next day, and, teaming that with my newfound, uninvited double Ds situation, she instantly said I needed to use a pregnancy test. In fact, she said she wouldn't leave until I did. This was her reaction to any slight bodily change since

I turned fifteen. So begrudgingly, I fetched a test – I already had one from when I'd had a similarly neurotic experience a while previously – and went to the loo, essentially just so that she would shut up and we could all get on with our lives and go to Caffè Nero for a too-hot panini.

Now, this is where things get blurry. My memory doesn't like this bit; it's not a fan of recalling the moments in that toilet – a defence perhaps Cheryl Cole also used. I also have no recollection of the three minutes I must have waited to see the results. I don't even remember doing the wee. I don't remember seeing the blue lines as they appeared, but I do remember feeling almost robotic, unlocking the door and passing the wee-covered stick to my mum who definitely saw the blue lines. 'Oh darling,' she said. Actually, I wish she had said that – in fact, think more: 'Oh for fuck's sake, Amy, it was only a matter of time.'

At that point, my neighbour, who to my poor mother's confusion just happened to be going through gender reassignment therapy at the time (yep, just like our hamster), came tumbling in through the unlocked front door saying something about leaving her phone at the party. 'OH HI, SOPHIE! HOW ARE YOU? COME IN, THIS IS MY MUM!' I gabbled enthusiastically, thinking that if I grinned hard enough then this situation would become all about Sophie's lost iPhone and my mum's inability to use correct pronouns – and no longer about me not being me any more. Because I wasn't just me, any more, was I? If this stick was believed to be true then I was PREGNANT me – and to become me again I would either have to HAVE A BABY or take all sorts of scary, adult action to make it go away. And both of those options sucked. I would much rather have just found Sophie's iPhone in a pile of tinsel before going for a nice, normal cup of tea at Caffè Nero with my mum, who in this hypothetical situation wouldn't be looking at me like she hated me. I wondered at that point if it was too late to pass the whole thing off as an experiment with performance art? I suspected it was.

After about a million hours of not finding her iPhone – 'Maybe someone threw it in the light fitting?', 'Maybe, Sophie, I'll check later, I promise' – Sophie left and the two of us were alone again. Though now, depending on how you look at it philosophically, I suppose there were THREE of us. So what do you do when you need to escape the giant elephant in the room that's taken up residency in your uterus? You decide that the best thing to do in this situation would be to go to Brent Cross shopping centre. I'm still not sure why. Maybe we thought I'd be less pregnant in Barnet? Only my mum couldn't navigate to Brent Cross shopping centre and we ended up on the M1 to Leicester. She couldn't navigate because I'd just told her I'd done the exact thing she'd spent her life instilling in me NOT to do.

Since the day of my first period she'd been telling and retelling stories about her mate who got pregnant in the 1960s, was chucked out of Ireland and had to live in a bedsit in Palmer's Green. Like any good mum, she made sure to drill it into me how a baby is chiefly a form of modern-day enslavement guaranteed to not only end your career, but quite possibly your life. Throughout my teenage years, I'd be carted off to the family planning clinic to be equipped with everything and anything I could possibly need to ward off any potential fertilisation. I think she'd have fitted me in a chastity belt if she could. I wished she had. As pregnancy's chief opponent, it's really quite incredible that she herself ended up having three children and has never once lived in a bedsit or in Palmer's Green.

But when it came to me her views were unshakeable. I can still hear her drumming it into me as a teenager: 'Just DON'T end up pregnant. It's so easy these days to protect yourself; only someone really stupid would actually end up pregnant.' And she was right, it is bloody easy to protect yourself, but I somehow hadn't; I'd let her down and now I was stuck. My pregnancy was very much here and left to its own devices, a baby would be getting dumped off by the stork in about nine months' time, via my beloved vagina which would almost certainly suffer one of those third-degree tears. Which would serve me right for being such a chief idiot.

At this point, my brain just started playing the most relentless game of 'what if' imaginable. What if I have the baby and wish I hadn't? What if I don't have the baby and wish I'd had the baby? What if my tits actually explode? . . . Meanwhile, my mum continued to hear the sat nav in a foreign language and head us into the north. Some people reckon they feel angry in this situation; I know that because I Googled it. But why would I feel angry? The only person I could have been angry at was myself and my mum was certainly covering that base. I was more just incredibly panicked, as if I were having an extended anxiety attack. I felt like I was trapped in my own body, hurtling further and further away from the life I recognised. Normal seemed a very long way away.

And so, with the weight of all that shit on my shoulders, lost on a motorway somewhere near the Midlands, I just cried and cried. Wailed like a cow that's just had its baby whipped away, which is kind of ironic in the circumstances. Not nice, neat crying like Amanda Holden does on *Britain's Got Talent*, but rather the type of crying that makes you look like a punched panda with conjunctivitis. Where you need so much time to cry that you don't even have time to breathe and end up making that loud, staccato, gulpy noise instead.

My body was a prison, and I felt utterly trapped within it. I had lost control. This all sounds horribly dramatic now, but at the time it felt akin to being told I had a terminal illness. It was as if someone had said to me, 'You know your carefully thought-out life plan? Nah, have this instead.'

BUT I DON'T WANT THAT, I DIDN'T ORDER THAT. SEND IT BACK TO THE BLOODY KITCHEN.

'Shut up, you're having it.'

Up until the actual whole 'living it for myself' bit, I really did think it would be as easy as just sending it back to the kitchen. Hit reverse, tell yourself it's just a ball of cells and then reassemble for original life plan part one. Maybe #shoutmy-abortion on Twitter before pitching a cautionary first-person confessional to The Pool. 'If I ever DID get pregnant . . . well, I wouldn't be pregnant for long,' I remember saying to Lorcan one day a few years earlier. I was certain I'd hit delete.

As it turned out, for me, it definitely wasn't as easy as that, and it was time to buckle in for some true emotional trauma, super-charged by all those delightful pregnancy hormones circulating my now shared body. Sitting in the car, my mind still frantically racing, I thought out a list of ways that this baby, this little person, could negatively affect my life enough to risk possible long-term regret and a lifetime of very expensive therapy sessions:

Realistically, I'd probably have to move home for a bit. Bin off 'We Have It All Fridays'.

My grandad would have to know.

I might get a wonky vagina.

My mum would have to tell her friends, who would act all concerned but secretly feel relieved that it was her daughter and not theirs.

I'd have to quit smoking and drinking with immediate effect.

And that was all just for starters.

Up until then, I felt like I'd only ever done things to make my parents proud of me. I'd got the good GCSE results, an all right degree that wasn't in sports science. They could tell their friends that I'd interviewed Simon Cowell – albeit asking him what brand of toilet roll he uses. Even though I smoked and didn't have a TV licence, I was – for the most part – a success story for the family name. But now I felt like the 'problem child' who had very much fucked up.

There were two choices here, and neither one was right or wrong – I wished there was a definite answer, but there wasn't. Instead, I had to wait a very long nine months for that. Don't worry; I've got it now. But then, all I had was just a load of working-out paper and no answer.

Slowly, alongside all the immediate panic and fear, some thoughts started to emerge about the possibility of keeping the baby. After all, having had a particularly, er, hedonistic early twenties – I definitely did have it all – I'd already had all the drinks and bad men I could scrape from the bottom of the barrel so I knew I could deal without the pubs and clubs. This lifestyle also meant I hadn't slept properly since 2005, so I was used to the whole not-sleeping situation. Perhaps, actually, I'd been having too much fun and it wouldn't be a bad idea to take this opportunity to grow up – even though I appreciated that motherhood was a bit of a dramatic means of fast-tracking into adulthood. I spent way too much time in my own head, so maybe it would be good for me to shift and share my focus with someone else? And I'd already finished all the studying I needed to do; I wasn't destitute; I would still have the same skills, talents and carefully curated wardrobe of fancy dress costumes. I would still be me.

Then there was the fact that my relative youth could actually be seen in a positive light. My mum was forty-two when she had me and although I wouldn't change my family for anything, I'd always been super-conscious I would have less time with her than my friends would with their mums. I was twenty-four and having a baby now would close the gap.

But the PLAN – oh, the precious, carefully carved life plan – it didn't go like this. The order was work another ten years, meet someone worth breeding with, marry them and bear their children. Repeat. Grow old together. The plan was definitely not work for a bit, have a weird fling with someone completely unsuitable, have his baby, future TBC. No one went off-grid when it came to life. If I went off plan, I'd almost certainly be poor and miserable.

But then – my racing thoughts flipflopping again – was this all about me? Or was it now about someone else – a little stowaway who had somehow made it all the way to a beating heart? After all, plans could be changed and postponed. And like those signs in the B&M home store (my fave) were always telling me: life begins when you are busy making other plans. Why DID unplanned have to automatically mean unwanted? Perhaps I actually wanted this deep down – I'd just never considered it. Now I had seen for myself that you really don't know what's around the corner, what life is about to chuck at you – so what if this was my one chance to be a mother? I'd always wanted to be a mum but always worried I'd never deem a time 'right'. But is there really ever a 'right' time? Would I ever really feel settled enough or be ready to take a career break? Surely every journey into motherhood comes with its own challenges; there is no perfect 'one time fits all'. And it's not always as simple weighing up whether your job, relationship and experiences are exactly where you'd like them, as there's also the very real possibility that pregnancy won't come when you want it. The universe obviously thought that this was the right time so perhaps there really was no time like the present?

Really though, my final decision just boiled down to me feeling that what was done was done and for me, it was too late to intervene. It's a woman's individual decision and I think I had made mine while I was still sobbing in that car going the wrong way up the motorway. No deep moral objections, no politics; I just sided with my own personal instincts. If the circumstances were different, I may well have chosen otherwise. But in that moment, for me – it was the choice I made.

Eventually, Mum remembered how to drive and we made it back to her house where, sitting in the kitchen I grew up in, I carried on wailing like a cow. I looked at my mum and knew what was going to come out of her mouth: 'Look, let me help you make an appointment, and we'll get this taken care of, OK? Don't worry about this. It will be like it never happened.'

This is what I expected her to say. Instead my mum squeezed my hand and said: 'Look, don't do it if it's going to break your heart.' My lovely mum was definitely very lovely in that moment, and at long last the wailing turned into more of a light snivel. My situation said 'have the baby', my gut said 'have the baby' – or maybe it was the actual baby which was pretty close to my guts at this stage . . . Either way, for me, right then, at that moment my decision was confirmed.

Mind now made up, I was surprised by how ashamed I felt. Having an unplanned baby is basically like walking around with a sign saying 'I CAN'T EVEN DO SEX RESPONSIBLY', in a world where it is SO easy to do responsible sex. Thank you, Durex. I felt embarrassed to be so self-indulgent as to actually HAVE a baby – like something off *Teen Mom* or like I was Sarah-Louise Platt in *Corrie*. I knew that most people would think that the right and sensible thing to do in my situation would be to terminate. I even knew people who had had terminations – but I didn't know anyone who had been so reckless as to actually bring an unplanned baby into the world.

My embarrassment was so real that I started (and sometimes still do) lying about the number of weeks pregnant I was, just to avoid it looking like it was my decision to keep the baby. For the record, I was eight weeks when I found out . . . OK, I was seven. I have said I was anything up to *twenty* weeks just to make sure people say, 'Oh wow, you didn't really have a choice then.' 'I even had periods!' I will always add – just so they can't catch me out. A selfish move on my behalf, because this also instils terror into all women, who instantly believe that they are a ticking pregnant time bomb. This does sound really awful, but not having an abortion was – in my head – a very unpopular decision. I was afraid people would think it was the ultimate spoiled brat move, as I was in a privileged enough position to be able to get away with it. I felt like I shouldn't be able to be happy about the decision.

It definitely surprised people. I was once interviewing one of the main characters from *TOWIE* when I was seven months pregnant, and he ended up finding out a bit about the circumstances. Rather bluntly, he asked: 'Sorry, but why didn't you just have an abortion?' Which, if I'm being honest, is probably what I would have thought – though perhaps not said – had I met pregnant me before this whole thing happened.

I'd surprised myself. The decision was supposed to be obvious. But then the stomach flutters, the morning sickness, the massive boobs . . . it was all so real. I know it's normal to have 'mixed emotions' even when you are *trying* for a baby, or so I hear, but this was next level shit. This was definitely: 'THIS stuff is normal, but if you are experiencing THESE symptoms, we advise you to contact a health professional', and mine were very much in the latter category. So I did – in fact I spoke to Marie Stopes on the phone so much during the first week or two that I considered sending the call handler flowers to say thank you. For those of you who haven't had to Google 'abortions near me', Marie Stopes provide support, services and treatments to women who find themselves pregnant when they didn't intend to be. And not just the ones that decide against the idea of having a baby.

For the next few weeks, my mind was experiencing the pregnancy equivalent of bipolar – one day I was genuinely excited and couldn't wait for this new chapter in my life, which was good because it was definitely on its way, and the next, I would be on the phone to the Pre and Post Natal Depression Advice and Support charity (PANDAS). PANDAS' helpline convinced me I had antenatal depression. One day I would be almost enjoying researching baby names or looking up whether the baby was the size of a grape or a pea. The next I would be crying – perhaps more accurately howling – to Lorcan that I felt my body had been invaded by a parasite like something in *Men in Black* (sorry, Freddy of now, my beautiful little alien). I'd grow convinced that even if people did forgive me, there was no way that they would ever forgive the baby for turning up unannounced. In my darker moments, I was sure my family were slapping a smile on for my sake, secretly hating this unborn soul for inflicting such chaos on to them. Essentially, I thought everyone had Freddy down as a womb terrorist. As it turns out, as the pregnancy progressed, they really were just excited to meet their new family member. However, paranoid pregnant me was convinced they were all just really good actors.

It had become clear that there was nothing single about my pregnancy. It wasn't just my life changing – it was everyone's around me too and I wasn't convinced then that the changes were welcome. I battled with relentless internal guilt that I'd messed up not only my life, but theirs too. Not to mention their reputation down the golf club. At one point, I even considered faking my own miscarriage so that I could change my mind and no one would have to know. The next day, I phoned my mum saying how devastated I would be to lose my baby. They don't mention THAT on the BabyCentre app. A Clear Blue advert it wasn't, as my hundred or so calls to the very patient professionals at Marie Stopes would have told you. For this reason, it was hard to know which way I really felt. However, by the end, it almost felt like this was my plan – well, apart from the whole moving back in with my parents aged twenty-four part – and really, who's to say it wasn't? Maybe, just maybe, this had happened for a reason. A reason I wouldn't be entirely sure of until the end of those nine months. Although I still maintain that it couldn't have happened to anyone more young and fabulous.

## 2

# KNOCKED UP WITHOUT THE HOLLYWOOD ENDING

I didn't expect him to want me; I didn't anticipate that. But I did expect him to want his baby. I didn't expect him to leave his son fatherless, to start off his life parentally lopsided. I met Freddy's dad, let's call him Barry, at a birthday party which he ended up gatecrashing – like father, like son in that respect. I say 'met' but we knew each other years before, although we were never really friends. He was one of the cool boys, the sporty boys and I wasn't exactly in that clique. I wasn't at a massive social loss during this time, just somewhere in the middle, never admitting but secretly wishing I could get a cool jock boyfriend. It pains me right in the soul now to realise that at that birthday party I morphed back into that former teenage self and couldn't believe my luck when he showed an interest. Sorry, me of now, but it's true. We started seeing each other every so often after that and I was smitten. Or perhaps, more accurately – I was obsessed.

I have a theory that you can be pretty successful in all areas of your life, but sometimes one thing has to give. My area of shortcoming was – at this time – men. Well, this man anyway. I warn you now; this is not a version of myself that I look back on proudly. This is the *Broadchurch* series two version of me – a blip in an otherwise acceptable track record of self-respect.

To me, Barry was charismatic, exciting, spontaneous, and looked exactly like Kit Harington. To everyone else he was a bit of a livewire who looked like Kit Harington if you got very drunk, then drank some more and put on someone else's prescription glasses. Writing about him now, I warm with genuine embarrassment about how I behaved when it came to this relationship – not that it is even worthy of the 'relationship' tag, if I'm being honest.

So what was it? If you were being kind (or American), you could say we were 'dating' – in that we spent intermittent periods of time together on a fairly regular basis – but that would be nothing more than an attempt at romanticising what was basically this: he made me feel so desperate that I chose happily to be his fuck toy over nothing at all. What we shared was a curious tryst of physicality that I longed to turn into something more.

My colleague used to tell me that who you date is a reflection of what you think of yourself. I obviously thought very little of myself; in fact, I must have regarded myself as an utter arsehole.

For the purposes of writing this chapter I read over our text messages from around this time and I am over him like a mad rash. I don't remember being SO desperate but you can't argue with the WhatsApp archive. I repeatedly ask him when he's free while he rattles off false excuses. He would say things like 'let's play it by ear' and in between these messages he would turn up at my house after he had been out drinking and not managed to pull during power hour. Taylor and Burton, it was not. One time I asked when I would see him next and he told me 'November' – it was August.

But emotionally invested I very much was. Elizabeth and I were totally on the same page in that respect. I don't think that I was ever in love with him, but sometimes infatuation can make you as mad as actual love and this boy, he definitely made me very mad. So mad that I wouldn't always be totally insistent about condoms when he complained men don't like them. He seemed pretty up to speed with the ol' ovulation cycle – albeit a rather Catholic approach to contraception – so, somewhat mentally, I did trust (or did I just want to trust?) we were in the 'safe zone'. I was my own personal Natural Cycles app and I thought we had it sorted.

It makes me uncomfortable to admit this now but he could have said anything and I would have believed it if I thought there was a possibility it might make him like me more. Pathetic, yes, but I was well and truly dick-matised. It's probably becoming clear now to you that he didn't seem to overly respect me, mainly because he didn't give two hoots about me as a person rather just occasionally having a fleeting affection for my vagina when all the others were closed. However, that didn't stop me going back time and time again, letting him use me and my Uber account to get him to my doorstep more than once. I even have the Uber receipt from the night I guess was the conception.

A month in, it even turned out he had a 'sort-of' girlfriend who he was 'sort of' still seeing 'but not really, if you know what

I mean'. Still I couldn't get enough of the weekly humiliation. I was like a love junkie looking for their next fix. After about two months I finally managed to wake from this temporary insanity, smell the damn coffee, realise he wasn't actually Kit Harington and begin to try my hardest to detox myself of him. With varying levels of success, I'll admit.

In fact, my success rate could be totally aligned to my alcohol intake. When I was pissed, I was weak and a hundred times more likely to make contact. I tried deleting his number, removing him from social media and blocking him on Facebook – the works. But where there is a pissed will, there is a way and I realised that I could scroll through old Facebook messages to find his number and Bob's your uncle – he'd be back for one night only. And in the morning, I would hate myself and start the whole sorry detox again.

To try and spur myself on in my journey, I wrote a list of pros and cons. There were seven pros to twenty cons. Pros included 'nice voice and face' and cons included 'never initiates conversation', 'quite often unemployed' and 'rude'.

When I found out I was, as my dad put it, 'in the pudding club', I hadn't seen him for about three weeks and was making real progress in my bid to kick this addiction. I had even started seeing someone new who actually seemed to like me a bit. So at the time I was already very much not in a couple with Barry and didn't expect that to change even as pretty much everything else, physically and mentally, was starting to do so.

Now some people here might jump to the conclusion I must have got myself pregnant on purpose – tricked this poor inno- cent chap into baking a bun in my oven. But believe me, I just wanted a boyfriend, not a baby. I wanted to be a TV presenter not a mother. To me then, those two things were very much not compatible so a baby was the last thing I would want to magic into my body. But I suppose what I *am* trying to make clear is that Freddy was never in the running to have a stable family unit; there was more chance of pigs flying over his birthing suite or me having a home birth (Christ, can you imagine?) than Mummy and Daddy ever actually being a typical mummy and daddy. But I didn't stop to think for a second that there wouldn't be both a mummy and a daddy. But then again, no one expected Leo to die at the end of *Titanic*, either. Didn't make it any less sad though.

After the whole two blue lines Brent Cross shit show, I knew it was just a matter of time before I had to tell Barry. I still didn't know what the hell I was going to do about this whole 'keeping it' situation nor did I yet understand quite what a fecal (or rather fetal) hurricane was going on in my body. I toyed with the idea of just never telling anyone who didn't already know, wearing very baggy clothes and then giving birth on the toilet before selling my story to a weekly women's magazine. That way I could pay for me and the baby to move somewhere no one knew us – like Jersey. Perhaps the government would even give me a new identity and I could start a new life under a pseudonym. Maybe something ironic like Mary? We could live in a stable too, nice and cheap, shabby chic. No one would ever have to know. It would be like the modern-day equivalent of packing myself off to a mother and baby home in the 1960s, only with less laundry. That way at least I wouldn't have to ever tell my now dead, then very much alive grandad. Well,

I'd managed to keep my tattoo a secret from him up until that point.

But ultimately, as a resident of the actual world, I knew that it wasn't just me; there were two people who had created the source of these relocation plans and so two people had to know. This was very much a shared ownership situation – a joint baby bank account – so I could hardly just cart the assets off to Jersey and get away with it. Plus, a problem shared is a problem halved, right? Whoever said that has definitely not had to tell their ex-boyfriend ('boyfriend' admittedly a bit of a stretch) who hates them (definitely not a stretch) that they are sort of pregnant. Well, not sort of – definitely pregnant.

There are fewer dramatic words you can say to a bloke than 'I'm pregnant'. It's pretty up there with 'I'm leaving you for your sister', or 'I've booked us musical theatre tickets', so yeah, you could say I was nervous. So what do people do when they want to minimise emotional upheaval? Do it on the phone. The theory being it wasn't WhatsApp, so it was the decent thing. Plus, I couldn't bloody face waiting for those two blue ticks to appear to show he'd read my message. I'd seen enough double blue lines recently.

Feeling like I was starring in my very own Richard Curtis film rather than my own ACTUAL LIFE, I called him and told him: 'I'm pregnant.' I understand now the importance of adding the 'and I'm keeping it' bit but in this instance I didn't quite manage it. The silence was just there, like a big gaping hole of awkward. So being me, unable to stomach silence in any capacity, I jumped in and filled it with what I knew he wanted to hear. 'I mean, I'm going to sort this out.'

Sort this out? Sort it out like a disorganised wardrobe. Chuck what I don't need out, make a bit of space – a good old womb clear-out, that's all that's needed here – and all would be back to normal by the morning. He finally said something. 'OK great, I'll come with you, and look after you.' He couldn't have sounded more relieved – I'd given him verbal Senokot. This was probably the most attention he had paid me ever, so being the feeble wench I was, I replied, 'OK, thank you, don't worry, I'll sort it out.'

'Thanks for being so good about all this,' he said, and we hung up.

As you know, I had no real intention of sorting anything out, but in keeping with the role I had fast cooked up I arranged an appointment at a Marie Stopes clinic – basically the Marie Kondo of disorganised wombs – and the next day I found myself slinking out of my office at lunchtime to go and discuss my 'options'. I expected to see a wall of protestors holding up plaques of dispelled foetuses screaming 'MURDERER' in my face, but instead the clinic could have been mistaken for a town house, with a big front door and a doorbell you had to ring to be let in.

Abortion clinics are funny places. They're like a doctor's surgery where everyone knows what each other is in for. There were older women, young women, women in sports gear, women in work clothes. Women crying, women reading magazines, women scrolling through their phones pretending not to notice the women crying. The only thing we all had in common was that we had somehow ended up there. But the main thing I took home was that there were A LOT of women.

As I sat in the waiting room, I thought more about my 'options', which felt increasingly more limited. I'd already decided I was just biding my time, and wasting Marie's, but that experience in the clinic did help to reaffirm what I already knew – I couldn't see a reason not to have this baby. 'Most of the ladies that we see are mums already, and can't finance another member of the family,' the nurse told me. And well, I had plenty of money, I wasn't a teenager, and like my dad said to me, 'What's all the panic about? We're talking about a BABY here.' News which was reconfirmed when I was scanned to see how developed my pregnancy was.

As the nurse put the jelly on my stomach, I felt like my life had hit fast forward. How the hell had I ended up here? Things were all out of sync. This was supposed to happen with me holding hands with my husband, eager to marvel at what we'd created, what we'd been wanting to create – the next logical step in our ordered lives. After two comes three – after wedding comes baby. Instead, I was on my own, mentally working backwards from the number of weeks I was being told – which took me back to the night of my work Christmas party. The night I'd drunk ALL the wine, called Barry up and turned up in an Uber having lost my shoes. That's not how people make babies. Only apparently it was and now I was staring at it on the screen. Well, trying to – in reality I was staring at the grainy screen and thinking how it just all looked like one big black hole and not much else.

'Would you like to know if there is a heartbeat?' the nurse asked me.

I'd already made my decision so 'Why not?' I thought – and like that, the nurse confirmed there was a heartbeat. Apparently, that meant my chance of miscarriage was really low. I didn't know whether I was relieved or terrified to hear this news. Maybe because I was actually a bit of both. I decided to keep the picture of the scan against the nurse's suggestion not to. In all the autopilot panic, I didn't realise I had technically 'gone private' by booking directly with a Marie Stopes clinic and the receptionist had to dash after me to ask me to pay. As I punched in my PIN, I imagined the receptionist thinking, 'What a truly careless idiot she is.'

The next day, I told Barry: 'I can't do this, I've changed my mind.'

There was no silence this time. 'Yeah, I think it's important we meet as soon as possible,' he answered in a fraction of a second.

Quick to appease him at any cost, I said, 'OK, I'll come over after I've finished work – I should be able to get there about six.' I could cancel my plans later, this was more important.

'I can meet you, but can we make it eight? The football's on.'

I kid you not, dear reader.

'Oh, and can you pick me up? The boys are at mine and I'd rather not have to do this with them in the house'

He could make a baby but he couldn't independently navigate himself from Crouch End to Golders Green

Now here you may be pondering whether it was right that I made that decision on my own and chose to leave Barry with no choice but to deal with it. This is a question I have agonised over – after all, who was I to chuck him under the speeding train of parenthood? Bastard or not, he would be affected by my decision. There was a baby with his DNA growing inside of me. To completely disregard the other progenitor of the unplanned pregnancy would have been narrow-minded and well, a bit mental. Of course, he was affected, emotionally too. However, he did have the sex, he did take the risk and now this was the consequence. If it were in his body, I would be at his mercy. That didn't mean I felt any less guilty. But by this time, after that scan, that heartbeat, I saw another person who wasn't me in this mess too. So now it was two against one and soz but majority rules. The situation also happened to have taken up residency in my body, so I also think that gave me the edge.

We arranged to meet after work. Well, I was working, he was probably at home looking in the mirror, masturbating and rolling cigarettes. I took a little longer than planned to get home from work that day after falling asleep yet again on the tube. I had not previously appreciated that pregnant women basically have narcolepsy. In between dozing, I imagined possible outcomes of the imminent meeting with my babyfather.

While clarity was never his strong point, Barry had always been clear about one thing – his relationship with his dad. He had told me that they were mega close. I remember once I had stayed over the night before he was meeting his dad for lunch and he got into a frenzy about being on time. Careful to highlight what a dutiful son he was with such excellent family values, he said, 'I would NEVER be late for my dad,' clearly irritated as I fumbled to find all my things in the impossible amount of time he had given me to get out his house. I think he ended up leaving the house ahead of me that day to make sure there was no possibility he would even be two minutes late to meet this much-hallowed father figure. Comparing this story with the current situation in my head I concluded to myself that there was no way Barry would allow a person to grow up without a dad on his account. Looking back, he probably just didn't want to have to talk to me on the walk to the tube station.

I expected a fairly explosive initial reaction but was certain also that there would be a calm after the storm. An acceptance not for me, I knew that ship had sailed – well, hardly sailed, it had never set sail in the first place – but for the future person at the heart of all this. The person currently making me feel ready to either vomit or fall asleep at the wheel of the car I was now driving to pick up the man equally responsible for his existence.

I had said I would get us dinner (implying civility) but I ended up not having enough time so had grabbed two microwave meals from the petrol station on the way over to pick him up. There was only one macaroni cheese left, so I had to buy fish pie – easily the Howard Donald of microwave meals. Although he did have a bit of a renaissance period so perhaps we can expect this of fish pie too. I digress.

Of course, Barry wasn't outside already – well, who knows what important sporting fixtures might have cropped up? – so I texted him to let him know that I'd arrived, and after about five minutes he appeared at the passenger door and got in. This was not exactly carpool karaoke, and I don't even remember what we talked about, but I do remember that the person who had wanted to hold my hand and accompany me to the abortion clinic – well, he had been replaced by someone very different indeed.

I drove him back to my flat and when we got there we sat in the living room and I told him all the pacifying stuff I'd heard people say on the telly in these types of situations. I told him that me having this baby wouldn't change us, it wouldn't alter what we could do, that he could have as little or as much contact as he liked. He told me that he had to go outside 'for a smoke'.

While he was outside, I pierced the film of the microwave meal – in the light of the circumstances I decided I would have the fish pie – and put it on. As the microwave pinged, he was gone, having escaped unannounced out of the back gate. In the time it took to reheat two Esso petrol station ready meals he had made his decision very clear. In the hope that actual digestion would help me digest what had just happened, I ate them both. I wasn't just eating for two, I was eating for all bloody three of us. Now the person who wanted to take the day off work was well gone, truly disappeared. Oh, actually, he did text later that evening, presumably after he managed to work out the bus route for his return journey. He'd left his bag of baccy on my patio table and asked if I'd keep it for him. Does that count? I wish I'd given him the fish pie. By this time, any feelings I had for him had truly disappeared. The former magnetic forcefield around him had somehow deactivated. It had been replaced by a searing protectiveness to prioritise what was going on inside me over anything else. Well, I think it was this. But it also coincided with me going teetotal.

A couple of days after the hasty exit over the back gate, I received a phone call from his mum, despite having previously never spoken to her in my life. Well, it had never been serious enough to 'meet the parents'. But now, things had become very serious, very quickly, so they had been summoned. And now here I was, awkwardly opening the door to my child's supposed grandparents, along with a sheepish-looking Barry, not knowing whether to shake their hand or kiss them on the cheek. In the end I sort of patted the mum on the arm and asked them if they would like a cup of tea. No one would like a cup of tea.

Barry sat the furthest away from me and kept his head down. Like most decent parents of their generation, his mum and dad had probably hoped they'd done a good enough job in raising a child who would avoid situations like these. In ordinary life, they would have been standard inoffensive parent types, prob-ably of a similar ilk to mine – in fact, we probably would have all got on just great. But planted in this scenario and I felt like the devil incarnate who had come up from hell to steal their son's sperm and ruin all their lives. I wished I could buy his mum a Boden scarf to make it all go away and she could thank me and say how 'funky' it was. I could see that, like me, they were terrified. I don't think anyone in that room knew how to deal with the situation. I still think it's sad they couldn't just take a risk and be open to a possibility that they most likely never thought they'd have to even imagine. But they couldn't. So that was that.

'Look, I don't want to be with your son. But this baby is coming, so it's up to you how involved you all want to be,' I told them, willing them to leave my house. The mum responded by asking why I had ever been with him in the first place. 'Well, he's really good at sex,' I told her. Surely that would get them to leave my house? Her face dropped as if she'd just found out there was no fennel left at the Waitrose deli counter. At this stage it was all getting a little middle-class Mafia, but I told myself that if Susanna Reid can put up with sitting next to Piers Morgan every single morning then I could hold my own in this situation.

It turns out I couldn't hold my own. Twenty minutes into this excruciating meeting, I put in a call to my own parents, who arrived on the scene impressively promptly. Mainly because I'd asked them to camp out up the road in case they were needed. Now, this really was what it would have been like to have had a teenage pregnancy. Only, we weren't – we were twenty-four, self-sufficient (ish) and we even bought and cooked our own microwave meals. WE PAID COUNCIL TAX, FOR GOD'S SAKE! It felt like that *Comedy Central Roast* TV show and I was the roastee, with the mum and dad taking it in turns to tell me why I should definitely not have this baby. Why it was quite possibly the worst idea in the history of bad ideas and it was likely to prompt nuclear war and the subsequent end of humanity and, indeed, the world. Things like:

'Barry's not ready for this, it will ruin his life.'

'Do you know the rates of death during childbirth?'

'Do you know what it feels like to be the odd one out of a family?'

'Weren't you DRINKING before you found out?'

But they were careful to stress, with every veiled persuasion tactic to eliminate the situation, 'Honestly, we are ultimately thinking of you, Amy.'

Their schtick was very much angled to the idea I had sin-gle-handedly stolen their son's sperm and that he didn't have an iota of responsibility. At one point, his mum checked to see if he needed to go outside 'for some air, darling'. Looking back, I should have used this intermission to quickly quiz them about any hereditary illnesses or family cancers that I might need to be aware of, so I could suss up their genetic credentials a little more thoroughly. But I was too emotionally exhausted by this point to think on my feet.

After going round and round the merry-go-round of reasons why I should change my mind another fifty times, eventually my own mum piped up: 'It's clear what you want and it's clear what Amy wants so I think we should end it here.' They shuffled to the door and before they left I grabbed his mum's arm once again and said: 'I'm really sorry that we had to meet like this.' And I was.

After the strange parental summit meeting, I didn't see them again. I still thought, in my heart, that after this rough start they would come round to the idea. That his mum would come round with a neatly packed baby basket from that JoJo Maman Bébé shop, saying how sorry she was for how we first met. How she was just worried and scared (weren't we all?) but now willing to support her grandchild even if he wasn't. Why! Well, because they had been adults way longer than us so I naïvely assumed they would be more familiar with the difference between right and wrong.

That never happened. Instead I received an email from Barry. It said that he didn't want his name on the birth certificate or to be involved in any way. He said this would benefit all three of us. He added that he didn't want any child seeing conflict so by scarpering he would be doing everyone a favour. Looking back, perhaps he was right. I am, believe or not, civilised. I make microwaveable fish pies for people I can't stand. Maybe my reasonable side can see he had a point? However, then I was full of pure venom, convinced that he was in the wrong.

Also, my eyes were drawn directly through this very dubious reasoning to the bit where he mentioned his withdrawal of 'all financial support'. That's the bit I still question today – how he got to the end result of NO forking out. He said he had only just worked out how to look after himself and so couldn't possibly look after a baby. He was twenty-four. He ended by saying that he just couldn't have a child he would have to hand over to someone else and as a result he didn't want to know anything about it – before requesting I never contact him again.

Now that email, it really was a punch in the tits. I was well and truly blindsided. There were so many things about it that took my breath away. Reading it then, three months up the duff – a result of something we'd done together – it felt so short, it was so selfish, it was such nonsense. I couldn't believe anyone could know about let alone support him with this so I sent his mum a message saying: 'Having received your son's email, I just wanted to check you know his decision?'

Quickly she replied to say that they would be supporting his decision. Even after that email, I thought he'd be back to face up to the situation he had created with his magic baby-making potion. But he never did.

Since that email, I haven't heard from him again myself – and, like he requested, I never tried to make contact with him. But he did get in touch with my family. Two weeks after

Freddy was born my dad received a phone call from him. Opting for some curiously chosen sporting terminology, he said: 'Hi Rupert, just getting in touch to see what the state of play is?'

'The state of play remains the same, so you won't need to contact us again,' he told him. Nice one, Dad. I knew I loved you very much for good reason.

It would be three months until I would see him again. I bumped into him in a pub and he just looked through me as if we'd never met. Meanwhile, I felt like my world had fallen out my arse. Mainly, I was just shocked. Shocked and worried that this might prompt his curiosity to get in touch. I resisted a *TOWIE*-style drink-chuck in his face – mainly because I just felt so sad. But instead of sad for me, sad for him.

Back then, I was tempted almost every day to say, 'Cough up, loser', to contact the CSA and to rinse him for every penny, hit him where it hurts, etc. But I don't have any plans to. That would give him a link to Freddy that he could potentially use to his advantage in the future, and I want Freddy to know exactly what his decision was right from the start. I'm all very Destiny's Child 'Bills Bills Bills' about the situation. That's not to say I didn't fantasise about erecting a billboard with his stupid smug face on it announcing he was having a baby and inviting anyone who cared to come to a baby shower at his home address. I didn't because a) I'm not Glenn Close in *Fatal Attraction* and b) because now it wasn't just about me – it was about this tiny life inside me. And that was so much more important than any bloke ever could be.

There are days when I mourn Freddy's relationship with his dad. Days when I get so, so angry that he's stolen that possibility from Freddy, the innocent party in all this. But on days like that I just remember what the lady from Marie Stopes said on the phone when I found out I was pregnant. She told me, 'All a child needs to flourish is one person to love it.' And that, I could definitely do myself.

## 3

# WHAT GOES IN,
# MUST COME OUT

'd made my decision to leave things in the capable hands of
nature. But now, that all felt like a big ol' anticlimax. I think
as soon as I accepted I was having a baby, I expected the
stork to cough it up then and there. Instead, now a great big
stretch of nothing lay ahead. Nine months of limbo. Not yet
a mother, but also no longer myself. For now, I was a ticking
time bomb filled with an expanding human set for detonation
in nine months' time. In the interim all there was to do was
to fear the unknown and apply bio oil in loving memory of my
'hot' body. To quote Lord Tennyson, 'tis better to have loved
and lost perky tits than never to have had them at all.

I was exploding out of my own body like the Hulk. I was
multiplying in size faster than you could say post-surgery
Kardashian. In fact, by the end I was the width of all the Kar-
dashians piled together. In light of this body mass extension,
people would have questions, and soon. So I had to work out a
plan of who and what I was going to tell and, most importantly,

how long I could get away with dramatically pausing before delivering the news. I decided to aim for Davina early series *Big Brother* – not revelling in it too much but still maintaining enough suspense to make everyone feel suitably uncomfortable. My immediate family knew, as did Lorcan. But everyone else? Well, I'd have to start making some very awkward phone calls.

I'd been, well, pretty shitty at work. I'd bunked off more than once to cry down the phone to Marie Stopes, made excuses to head out for scans and on a couple of occasions had to panic-close 'signs of early miscarriage' on Google when I was supposed to be working out how best to interview Mark Wright. With all these goings-on, I knew I'd have to tell my bosses fairly sharpish. My editor at Yahoo had become more like a friend and I knew I'd be able to trust her to know first. As I could have predicted, she hid her surprise with a smile and assured me my secret was safe for as long as I needed. She also somehow seemed genuinely excited for me and I got the feeling that she knew more about this babymaking lark than she was letting on. Indeed, eighteen months later she became a mum to the most beautiful baby boy. She is as wonderful a mother as she was my boss.

I wish this could have been an indicator of everyone else's reaction. If you are in a relationship and tell people you are pregnant they (usually) say 'Congratulations!' When you are single and you tell people you are pregnant they say, 'But . . . you don't even have a boyfriend?' No I don't, thanks for the reminder, pals. In fact, no one said congratulations to me throughout my pregnancy – which is probably why I never dared think or say it to myself. Instead people just said 'oh my GOD' over and over again, switching the emphasis from the OH to the MY to the GOD with every repetition. If you know someone who has just found out she is pregnant, whatever the circumstance, ring her up right now and say congratulations, please. You wouldn't believe how wonderful it would have been to hear those words. I imagine, anyway.

Soon after I set about the task of telling friends, with most assuming I had a terminal illness and/or was moving to Australia when I texted to say 'I have some news'. Well, I definitely hadn't got engaged. The odd optimist thought I might have got a presenting job on actual telly. The radical pessimists thought I'd lost my job – alas, that wouldn't be for a while yet. But ALL thought I was joking when I first told them. Well, ha ha, the joke was on them because I was very much serious. Once they knew the truth, the reactions split into two camps: the people who couldn't believe I'd decided to keep the baby (sorry, Freddy, they were the rude idiots anyway) and the people who wanted to embark on violence against his biological dad. The first camp were very much convinced my life had come to a full stop, chiming in with things like: 'But, like, I just couldn't do it because I still have SO much to do' or 'Was it too late to, y'know, change your mind?'

Meanwhile, I decided to keep the news off my social media. If you weren't close enough to see me IRL in the next nine months, I didn't need to tell you. This is what I told myself but really, I was still embarrassed and felt revealing the news would be akin to uploading a photo of myself holding a sign saying 'I CAN'T USE CONDOMS PROPERLY' or 'SURPRISE! MY CAREER IS OVER!' I remember when I was quite visibly pregnant my mum and I went for lunch with my gran, who has since died. She said nothing other than she understood what had happened and was sorry I'd been let down but that I'd be just fine by myself. Then she asked me to pass the gravy. My mum sent her flowers the next day for being so kind. She later told me how Gran had accepted her as a single mum when she met my dad. She already had my two brothers from a previous relationship and my gran welcomed all three of them with open arms. (Although my mum also adds that she thinks that might have been partly to do with how keen she was to offload my 31-year-old notoriously badly behaved, part-time alcoholic dad.)

People say smells can transport you back to a time, but I can't recreate the supersonic smelling abilities of early pregnancy so I think my senses opt for audio. Whenever the song 'Hey Now' by the band London Grammar comes on, bile literally rises up in me prompting a sort of indie pop PTSD. My gag reflex isn't a fan of London Grammar. Speaking of which, neither was my soon-to-be birth partner Lorcan: 'I work in Chelsea, if I want to hear a posh woman wailing I'll just stick my head out the window, thanks,' he said. But back then I worked in Covent Garden with no such opportunity and I had their album on a loop around the time I accidentally made my baby. To me it was melancholic and dramatic and suited my awful relationship. When I put it on I channelled Romeo at the beginning of *Romeo and Juliet* when he gets chucked by Rosaline. I thought I knew drama then. I had no idea. Nowadays, the song just serves as an audible reminder of what it feels to find yourself expecting what you very least of all expected.

If I imagine a graph of self-acceptance from that time, the line plummets like the New York stock exchange in the 1980s. I can imagine Jonah Hill in *Wolf of Wall Street* facepalming as he gawps at it while dropping one of those phones from the eighties with the curly wires to the floor. I'd had my own Wall Street crash – in a moment everything had changed and no one had seen it coming. So was it any wonder I was taking a little bit of time to adjust?

Every time I went for a scan I would be asked the same question after revealing that I was single. No, the father wouldn't be present, I'd say. 'Oh but you know who it is, don't you?' they'd ask, sometimes joking, sometimes serious. I started to learn that most people, health professionals included, align accidental pregnancy with promiscuity. Single? Then celibate please, we're British.

During a late scan I had an experience which I'll struggle to forget. I was on my own that day and was seeing a private doctor; I was considering having a private obstetrician so I wouldn't have to carry on explaining myself to a million different midwives. As part of the appointment he offered to give me a scan to check on how things were progressing. During the scan he said, 'You know the sex, right?' to which I said yes, I did. 'Well, good because he's CERTAINLY a boy! Can I ask you a question?' he asked. I wish I'd said no.

'Was his dad black?' I double-checked that Bernard Manning wasn't in between my legs. Nope, still the shiny bald head of the doctor. 'Mixed race . . .?' he trailed off. When you are on your own, people say a lot more to you. Ill-timed racist jokes, included.

39

I wasn't, however, entirely on my own at this time. Somehow when I discovered I was going to have a baby, in front of my transitioning neighbour in that flat in Golders Green, I was actually in a new relationship. Having properly said 'see ya' to Barry the month before, I'd managed to meet someone. Still blissfully unaware I had a human stowaway, I had been seeing someone so grown up and proper that he had his own lovely flat in West London and a job in the City (he was a banker so also quite loaded and he actually took me to Nobu once). What's more, he was not a total arsehole to me. In fact he actually went against every stereotype that normally comes with a description that includes words like 'banker', 'City', 'Nobu'.

So of course, I wasn't very interested. I never was interested in men like that, 'that' being ones that my mum would actually like. I never felt up to their standards so would just bin them off as some sort of twisted act of self-preservation. But I was seeing him when I discovered I was harbouring another man's baby up my foof, which is not exactly love tonic, unless you are very niche – and I promise, it wasn't anything like that. Being actually quite nice and, like I said, not a total arsehole, he told me he liked me, he understood and he still wanted to carry on and try to 'give things a go'. Knowing I'd probably be hard up for options – unless I was willing to become a fetish – and wanting to honour his noble offer I agreed to keep things going as they were. I also remember the day we had that discussion was the day I discovered I could no longer wear an underwired bra, as my ribs had started to expand to make space for my internal plus one. I should have known that a boyfriend and a nursing bra are not compatible but in that moment I was more 'where there's a will, there's a way'. Or, as some might say: IN DENIAL.

'Maybe we could just eventually PRETEND the baby was his and all live happily ever after?' I thought as I moved the clasp on my Mothercare bra to the loosest setting. Obviously, that was never going to work, was it?

Diana reckoned there were three people in her marriage. Well, there were literally three in my relationship. And soon the knowledge of this became too much for this poor lad who had just signed up for a bit of a laugh with a girl with an empty womb. I mean, it wasn't much to ask. Unfortunately this womb would be engaged for the next nine months.

Bless this guy – give him a medal for services to his gender, perhaps – because he really tried. But as things became more noticeable, dinner dates became lunch dates and lunch dates became cinema dates until he eventually admitted defeat. I think he called things off with the old 'let's just be friends for now' – the 'for now' referencing my not-ideal personal situation.

'I just can't imagine nine months minimum with guaranteed no affection . . .' I whined to Lorcan after things properly ended, probably to the soundtrack of London Grammar wailing. 'Oh, love, don't you worry – that baby will definitely give you *plenty* of affection,' he replied. But knowing I was now officially romantically redundant made me obsess about what I hadn't got and wouldn't be in a position to be getting anytime soon. No dating, no snogging, no NOTHING. Even nuns don't have to deal with that PLUS baby weight.

This wasn't helped by the fact that pregnancy makes you really horny. Sorry to any family members reading this (especially Freddy) but we're all grown-ups here (and Freddy, if you aren't yet a grown-up – what do you think you are doing? Put the book down and get to bed). It's as if the world is trying to tease you, knowing full well how you got yourself in this situation in the first place. I was also too scared to masturbate in case Freddy could see me.

I've no doubt husbands who say they found their wives most sexy when pregnant are telling the truth. But as for men who aren't your husband or didn't make that baby, I totally excuse them for not being mega turned on by swollen everything (and I mean EVERYTHING – thanks to my waxer for letting me know that little titbit) and an inside-out belly button. I didn't have a husband to marvel at 'what my body was capable of' – instead I just had an absent ex who had scarpered as a result of discovering just that. It was unlikely he'd be crawling out the woodwork anytime soon to present me with gherkins and ice cream and to have sex with me while worshipping my femininity and wondering at my fertility.

For the first few months, my body did me a favour and saw off anything remotely eighteen-plus with a whiff of intense nausea or by cramming itself with salt and vinegar crisps – completely against my will, obvs. I suppressed my natural urges with fast food. But by the six-month mark I was in the mental market for some sexual healing. Apologies if you are eating lunch at the moment. So enter catfishing. 'What's CATFISHING?' I hear some of you say. For those of you whose adolescence didn't feature Nev and Max on MTV quite as heavily as mine, catfishing is using someone else's photos and pretending they are your own on online profiles – in my case Tinder. (As an aside, did anyone else really fancy Nev and Max? Oh. Er, me neither . . .)

To be fair, I catfished using my own non-pregnant photos so perhaps kittenfishing would be more apt. MTV, feel free to call me to discuss the concept further. In my pretend land, I wasn't the colour of dishwater and the size of an adolescent elephant with the appetite to match – I was still that girl in Ibiza 2010 (OK, 2008) and a CATCH, DAMMIT. So I would swipe right to prove I was still desirable, still young, still the same as I was before all this. After all, I *was* still single. I would chat with men until they tried to make an actual IRL date at which point I'd strangely never be free until fading out completely. Yes, this was unfair but probably not as unfair as actually turning up. As I had already learned, this was an extreme one even for the most decent of men. Although turning up all pregnant would provide them with the number-one online dating horror anecdote which could be told indefinitely. So at risk of becoming their stock answer to 'What's been your WORST date?', I just stopped talking and moved on to the next one.

I'd like to take this opportunity to apologise to any men who may have been disappointed, or whose self-esteem took a knock after being inexplicably ghosted during this time. But at least you can all take comfort from this if you've ever been ghosted in the past – it could be less to do with you and more to do with your Tinder date having a due date.

But eventually I did embark on an IRL relationship. I reignited an old fling from my past. Blame it on the hormones or just plain just – I'd been denying it for ages and pregnancy forced me to give in. HA, gotcha – I'm talking about chicken nuggets. Of course I didn't have a pregnancy boyfriend – although respect to anyone who is brave enough. Not that it was any less of a love affair – an intense nine-month whirlwind which I claimed was a result of 'pregnancy cravings'. I've been brought up by *Heat* magazine interviewing pregnant celebrities with the stock question, 'Ooh, what are your CRAZY cravings?' (see also 'How WILL you juggle it all?') followed by answers about boyfriends having to go to the garage at 4 a.m. for licorice and Five Alive. IMAGINE THAT, I thought.

Well, thanks to this knowledge of a societal expectation for me to eat like an insane person I didn't want to disappoint. So after twenty-four years of being on a diet and becoming a human calorie calculator I just, well, stopped. I wish I could be like Cheryl Cole and at times of stress *lose* weight and look all fragile and delicate. But when I'm stressed – and those days I was stressed – I eat my feelings. So that, coupled with the dietary free pass of pregnancy, I ate what I wanted, when I wanted. I was eating for two, as they say. It's true, I did have a craving for chicken nuggets but really, I always have a slight, dormant craving for chicken nuggets and instead of just denying it I honoured it. I honoured it for nine months. Till birth do us part.

I remember when Kim Kardashian got pregnant for the first time and an editor at Yahoo said people weren't fascinated just simply because she was having Kanye West's baby. They were fascinated 'to see this tiny woman exploding out of her own body'. Well, I was a Kim Kardashian pregnant person. In particular, the time she was compared to Free Willy when she wore monochrome. And I blame my repressed love of fast food restaurants. When I was pregnant I would eat two KFC boneless banquets in one sitting. That was lunch. My local Chinese – shout out Dragon City in Golders Green – knew me by name and would reserve me the 'nice table by the window'. Which also meant that passing commuters on their way to the station could marvel at the scoffing pregnant girl on her third round of crispy duck. Then I'd be surprised when I didn't feel like my Michelle Heaton pregnancy exercise DVD was being overly effective.

And of course, I still whined and moaned when I got off the scales two days after giving birth and was as heavy as two of my ex-boyfriends. But this wasn't baby weight. It certainly wasn't my self-control weighing anything down. Instead, it was the weight of the curse of the KFC colonel and his pesky secret recipe which I was seemingly on a one-woman mission to find out.

In fact, I'd go as far to say guilt-free KFC was the best part of single pregnancy.

The worst part, meanwhile, was three months of morning sickness. Which FYI, isn't just in the morning. It's all bloody day and hangs around like an incurable three-month hang-over. If you haven't been pregnant before and are wondering what morning sickness feels like just go out and have loads of REALLY cheap white wine, preferably from a Wetherspoons, pass out before having a bit more and then the next day you'll get a fairly accurate idea. Well, that's how early pregnancy felt to me anyway. Wowzers, did I feel sick. I clutched on to ginger root – ginger tea – ginger biscuits – anything ginger to ease the intense nausea. I would have chewed off the arm of Ed Sheeran to ease the pain.

Apparently, if you feel really sick then your womb lodger is more likely to be a girl. People would tell me this all the time.

So I started to imagine what kind of baby I would have and I became fixated on the idea that this was my path – I was going to have a daughter. It all made sense now. A boy could be like a teeny version of let's call him Barry – and that coming out from between my legs was a very terrifying prospect. I found comfort in my certainty that I was having a baby girl and would imagine me, the baby and my mum as a sort of Three Musketeer-type racket with people marvelling at our similarities. I could take her dancing and she would be better than I ever was and would win a scholarship to the Royal Ballet School. Our supposed chromosomal similarities eased my fear of motherhood – she was going to be a mini me so of course it would all come naturally. I even picked out a name, Erin.

So when I got to the twenty-week scan and they told me I was having a boy, I wasn't exactly chuffed. You know that face Jonah Hill made earlier in this chapter? Here he was making it again.

To my shame, I cried because I was having a boy. I'm sure the majority of people love and want their sons just as much as their daughters – but I was being mad. I couldn't play football, I didn't know the rules to rugby, cricket or, in fact, any ball game. I'd only learned to run when I was eighteen and even then I got sciatica because I did it too much like a ballet dancer. I'd be the worst mother to a boy. You must understand that the spectrum of gender doesn't apply when you are single, pregnant and freaking out. Basically, how could I raise a boy? I didn't even know what a wet dream technically is. Or are they just urban myths? Genuine query.

I felt like this boy couldn't possibly have a relation to me and would just be the male contribution to this situation in miniature form. The miniature form, like his larger counterpart, would surely resent me and want to know why he was stuck with just me, with whom he had absolutely nothing in common. I think, in my head, I actually birthed Barry there and then in the ultrasound room. It was irrational and founded on very little but perhaps being sure I was expecting a girl was my way of taking some control of my situation and being told otherwise took it away again. Once more, I was being given something I hadn't asked for. I left feeling I'd hit a diversion.

I would spend the next five months being irrational and ungrateful about my perfectly healthy and well-developing boy. If there is a next time, I won't be finding out a thing at the twenty-week scan. Have you ever heard of 'gender disappointment' following the actual birth? Didn't think so. But I forgive anyone else who goes a little bit West in the scanning room. I certainly did. There are loads of people who are secretly sad and it's totally normal.

The remainder of my pregnancy was shrouded in size sixteen clothes – I'd literally DOUBLED in size – and now only Primark patterned harem pants would do. It was summer and the Central Line was hotter than ever; I had the thigh chafe marks to prove as much. In a vain attempt to halt this dress-size mayhem I signed up to do baby yoga just round the corner from work. However, I stopped going after forgetting to take my yoga clothes to work for the third time in a row. Also, the teacher kept telling us all to tense our sphincters and I wasn't sure it was exactly for me. However, it was here I discovered that unicorns ARE real and I met another actual real-life pregnant single girl. Finally, I had discovered where they had been hiding – tensing their bum holes just off Drury Lane. Despite our best intentions, we didn't end up meeting up after our respective births but just knowing there were other people doing this on their own was a huge comfort.

I didn't join NCT – I knew I would be the only solo human bowling ball there. So although I secretly wanted to know the stuff they'd teach me, I decided I could Google what to pack in my hospital bag on my own instead. This meant I had no pregnant mates and just my normal mates who spent their time collectively surmising whether my vagina would still work post-childbirth. To be honest, I was pondering the same thing. Collectively, we concluded both I and my vagina were doomed.

Speaking of which, in July, I took a particularly misjudged trip to Lovebox (sounds like a fun word for vagina, right?) Festival. If you haven't heard of Lovebox, then allow me to set the scene for you: everyone there is under twenty-five, booty shorts are the unofficial uniform and it's definitely not one of those festivals with a family area. I had a free ticket through work and was determined that, pregnant or not, I was still young and cool enough to know who Skepta was. Well, I knew the name anyway.

I was sitting behind a table, bump out of sight, when two guys came over to me and my friend. I felt so awkward as I realised they were chatting us up that I just went along with the banter until they bid us goodbye. At which point the slightly fitter of the two slipped me his phone number. For a second, I felt like Ibiza 2008 Amy – maybe, just maybe, he knew my situation and he chose not to mind? We bumped into them (no pun intended) again later but this time I wasn't hidden, and he and his friend laughed at their mistake as if it was truly the funniest of all the jokes ever made in the history of comedy. He apologised to me and just kept on laughing and laughing at the hilarity of chatting up a pregnant woman. It was loud in the tent so we had to crane in to hear what they were saying so to help us out at one point he even gestured to his own belly and did an impression like that bit in *Bridget Jones: The Edge of Reason* where she tries to buy the pregnancy test. I felt a lot like a court jester when I was pregnant. Well, a baby bump is not like a spot you can just vaguely attempt to cover up with concealer. I was a walking weevil minus a wedding ring and everyone wanted an explanation.

I continued to try to cling on to my old life and actually took an eight-month-pregnant trip to Ibiza with Lorcan. I was so pregnant that we had to check with the airline they would even let me fly. By this stage, I weighed about five times our baggage allowance. We stayed on the family side of the island – but I still felt like the spare part amongst gaggles of women whose bikini contained just one person. Spending a previously unchartered amount of time in the actual daytime as opposed to our usual nocturnal Ibiza stints, Lorcan ended up getting sunstroke and had to leave dinner early to vomit in his hotel room. I felt like I'd ruined his time away by being so out of action. I couldn't drink, I couldn't smoke, I couldn't do any obnoxious clubbing or the stuff we were good at – what use was I to him? We could barely shout 'We have it all!' out the window any more. Unless you count ALL the sunstroke, I suppose. I have never said anything about that holiday until now and, of course, Lorcan sweetly maintains he had a good time. But my pregnant paranoia definitely remembers it differently to him.

One time I did actually go clubbing to prove I could still do it. Have you ever been out in your day clothes to a posh bar and noticed how people don't look at you quite the same? They sort of look through you, like you are invisible. I'd never realised how much I used my sexuality until I was taken away and replaced with someone with a gut like Homer Simpson and the sex appeal of an UGG boot. OK, there was a baby in there but I didn't really BELIEVE this then so instead I just felt really fat. People just looked at me like, 'What is a pregnant girl doing in a nightclub?' while eyeing my drink to weigh up whether they could take the moral high ground. Of course, I didn't drink. I've always hated dancing in clubs and have to be very drunk to do so. Someone saying 'COME ON! HAVE A DANCE!' seems to further weld my feet to the floor. The only thing worse than dancing in a club sober is dancing in a club sober and pregnant, so, after two excruciating songs on the dancefloor I got an Uber home. I gave it my best shot.

It was around this time that the social anxiety started to kick in. Sometimes PMT brings out the agoraphobic in me and parts of pregnancy felt like PMT turned up to max. I'd become a walking talking point at a time when I couldn't have felt less like talking. Lorcan celebrated his birthday with a party at our house and I spent the time feeling like someone else, someone who definitely wasn't me. Everyone there had their lives in order; their lives were sticking to their plans, the socially acceptable paths. A girl was talking about a promotion at work and as I looked at her thin body which went in and out in all the standard woman places, I felt like a practical joke in comparison. Her future was obvious; mine was a blur. While she was going forward, I felt like I was going backwards – especially seeing as it wasn't long before I would have to move home. Half way through I made my excuses and fled to my parents' house.

Yep, my cosy living situation was about to change. I was about to move in with my bloody – sorry, loving and supportive and thus amazing – parents. But hang on – young, cool millennials like me lived in East London in a converted warehouse, NOT in rural Hertfordshire with their mum and dad and no lock on their bedroom door. HOW COULD THIS BE? Well, let me explain: young cool millennials don't get preggo out the blue. So when I decided I would let nature take its course I wanted to think I could stay living with Lorcan in our two-bedroom flat. He wouldn't mind, I surmised. After all, we'd always joked that if we didn't meet any respective boyfriends by the time we were thirty then we'd just knock through the wall and have a baby together. Now I'd made the baby – so surely he would want to live with it? It would be like *The Next Best Thing* with Rupert Everett and Madonna. RIGHT? We already had a hamster and a frog so what difference would a baby make?

Lorcan didn't agree and, though I hadn't actually met a new-born baby at that point, even I guessed – based on the way people talk about them – that their lifestyle probably wasn't totally syncable with that of a twentysomething PR exec whose Twitter bio read 'bright lights, late nights'. It still didn't feel any less shit. I grieved us living together and it was then and still is the only thing I truly do miss about my pre-baby life. I know it never could have worked but that doesn't stop me wishing that it could have. Especially every night at about 9 p.m. when I switch on the telly and have no one to watch it with. It's not that no one is there – it's just no one else quite has the same unique telly taste as us. We are the people who rewatched ITV's *The Club* and did impressions of Sam Fox. We are the people who searched Princess Diana's *Panorama* interview on YouTube every Sunday. Living with anyone else is never going to be quite the same, that's just one of life's few certainties.

I also would have had very little money coming in and would have even less once I'd popped the baby out so, due to economic and social poverty combined, my parents let me move back in with them. Which is actually amazingly kind when you consider they'd just moved into their dream retirement house (N.B. not an old people's home). They'd literally just signed the papers when we found out the news of our soon-to-be youngest family member. My parents had decided to 'downsize' as me and my two brothers were 'long gone'. Well, SURPRISE! You've got yourselves a two for one deal, congrats! My mum had always dreamed of having her own walk-in wardrobe and at last they had the perfect space to convert a bedroom into her own Carrie Bradshaw-vibe space. She'd been on holiday to Orlando once and had interior design stars in her eyes. Well, that became Freddy's nursery. I was twenty-four, single, pregnant and now living in a walk-in wardrobe. I was WINNING at life.

I stayed living in my two-bedroom flat with my best friend and our Harry Styles cardboard cutout until the final week before I was due to give birth. Sadly, Snoop Frog had to be rehomed and now lives with a reptile enthusiast family in

Milton Keynes. Lorcan now lives in Bow with a couple who are yet to impulse buy a hamster. We all moved on to better things, I think.

Forget *Catastrophe*, a 23-year-old fabulous homosexual man living with a heavily pregnant singleton is a sitcom waiting to be written, as we were the most unlikely pair. But it worked and I owe that friend everything from this time. The hysterical days of coming to terms with my decision, the plots to fake a miscarriage (he just nodded and never judged), the months of hangover morning sickness, the intense nicotine cravings, bloody Valentine's Day . . . he stuck by me for the lot and it just goes to prove that you don't need a romantic relationship to feel comforted and whole – you just need good, trustworthy people. Lorcan is now Freddy's godfather and he even cut the cord when he was born – he says it was like cutting chicken skin. Yum.

I spent £200 on everything I would need to start my new life, partly because I'm poor but mainly because I spent my money on ASOS back then. Even though I was decking out the walk-in wardrobe and getting it ready for the baby I still didn't really, if I'm honest, believe it would actually come. Buying previously foreign objects like 'muslin squares' and a steriliser felt like the weirdest version of picking the pencil case with the protractor in Year 9. I had no idea what I was going to do with any of these things but I definitely felt very grown up indeed.

Shopping for everything on my own didn't feel strange as it's all I'd ever known, so it seemed normal. Pushing a pram, however, that didn't feel normal and I daren't even have a go – I just hoped I'd feel different once there was a baby in it. Putting together a room of flat-pack furniture, well, that also didn't come quite so naturally. I did attempt it but after an hour of trying to connect Part C to Fixing 3 and googling 'flat-pack furniture cheat' I called my dad for assistance. He then called a Romanian man called Paul. But apart from outsourcing the flat-pack furniture, I was so proud that I was making and preparing everything myself. Although I was back living in my parents' house, I was becoming a grown-up, finally.

I was also starting to become more and more aware I wasn't just myself any more. A baby moving inside you, I think, is a real edge women have on men. Experiencing this struck me completely unexpectedly. Now, recalling it is like waking up from a dream and trying to remember it. But I know that I loved it, and I know it made the pregnancy that much more real. I really WAS going to have a BABY. And he liked to remind me of this rather violently, usually in the early evening just in time to freak Lorcan out while we watched the worst (but best) TV. From a mere fetus, Freddy was a RuPaul fan. Whether it was a protest from within to stay tuned or he was just poking me to remind me this definitely wasn't pretend, the feeling of a baby kicking inside me is a memory I honestly cherish so hard and has a firm place in my mental memory box.

When I got that taxi home from that fateful nightclub where I was very much not like the pregnant woman off *Spice World*, I ran a bath. As I soaked in the special maternity bubble bath Lorcan had bought me to cheer me up the week before, I felt a chapter of my life close. However, for the first time, I could see the light of a new one opening. Just then a foot or elbow protruded from my belly like something off *Alien*, and my little alien and I were in sync and knew we were going to be all right. Even if we wouldn't be going clubbing together again until he was eighteen.

# 4

# RIP VAGINA

Frederick Rupert William Nickell was born at 10.01 a.m. on 10 September 2014 in Watford General Hospital, the day the iPhone 6 came out. I know this because it's the first thing my birth partner Lorcan told me after arriving at the hospital. When Lorcan turned up I'd already been in labour since the previous evening but my other birth partner – my mum – and I didn't see the point of waking him up when it became clear that Fred was in no rush to greet the world. I'd heard Davina McCall gave birth in a squat position in about an hour and decided that I would channel my inner Davina like a true warrior woman, impressing all with my stoic strength. Alas, it wasn't to be. In fact it all went a little off-piste after I made a rather questionable decision re. my birth plan.

Unlike Davina, I had decided to have an 'elected induction' – I wasn't overdue, I just paid a private doctor to yank my baby out on a selected day. Yes, you can do that if you have a reason – my reason was because I didn't have a partner I didn't want to get caught short in a wet puddle with no one to get me to hospital. You still give birth in a normal hospital but have a private obstetrician by the time you get to the grand finale. It was my mum who recommended this course of action, having had three babies this way with no complaints. However, things must have been different in the seventies and eighties because believe me, I won't be recommending it to anyone. Not even people I REALLY don't like.

In case you aren't gathering, just like so many things in 2014, Freddy's birth didn't exactly go to plan. I fathomed I'd done the hard graft, surfed the puke waves, battled through the expanding body mass abyss, done the pregnant clubbing until I couldn't see my own genitals any more – surely this would be the easy part. Oh, the dramatic irony.

On the morning of 9 September I arrived at the hospital to have the first pessary put in, designed to 'get things going', so to speak. For anyone unfamiliar with pessaries, think smear test but a very extreme one. Don't listen to anyone who says 'it's just like a tampon, really'. Hmm, yes, I can see what they mean. IF TAMPONS WERE MADE FROM DAGGERS, MAYBE. Then I was sent home to let it take action, which the lady assured me would be slow and steady. An excellent, timed and planned birth. What could possibly go wrong?

So me and my three cap birth hat-trick mother decided to go to Pizza Express in Watford. 'Now, THIS is labour,' I thought as I tucked into a La Reine pizza, thinking how everyone goes on so unnecessarily about it. 'More garlic butter please and do you have any fried chicken lurking out the back, perhaps? I've only one day left of eating for two, you see.' The general vibe of this lunch was very 'death row inmate last meal', with the aim to eat as much as possible while I still had time left. It was about 1 p.m. at this stage. I had loads of time to dine out off the old 'I'm technically giving birth RIGHT NOW' joke.

After Pizza Express we went to Boots to buy some snacks and magazines to take to the hospital later and I told the woman on the till I was in labour and laughed at how merry it all was. 'Ho, ho, ho, this birth lark is a BREEZE,' I thought. Then we hopped in the car and whizzed off home as things progressed. I sat down to watch some daytime telly when I started feeling a little niggle. A niggle that became more like a shooting pain, like it was just becoming apparent the curry I'd had the previous night was dodgy. The pain quickly transformed from dodgy curry question mark to period pains on steroids – and when the period pain on steroids struck I started making noises reminiscent of distressed cattle. I actually MOOED, at which point my mum berated my 'rubbish pain threshold' that I 'must have got off your father' and requested I 'go upstairs' so she could hear the telly properly. Upstairs, I decided to watch a documentary about the street children of Rajasthan in between mooing and thinking 'I wish I'd been born a man'. The physical excruciation was now matched by the visual images of the terrible plight of those poor children. Twenty minutes in I gave up, went downstairs and told my mum this couldn't be normal.

'I know, it's truly awful, isn't it? Just where are the parents?' she replied. Shaking her head she caught my eye as I was hunched over groaning. Only then did she clock I was, in fact, referring to my own internal drama rather than the plight of the children of Rajasthan. 'Oh right, yeah, well, we should probably get you to the hospital – ask the doctors what they think,' she quickly added. Reluctantly, she then drove me to the hospital. I made a mental note to donate more money to charity.

Having concluded that contractions are the deepest circle of hell, I hobbled into 'triage' where the nurses sort the men from the hypochondriac boys. When I told them what time my pessary had been fitted, the nurses gave me the similar Doubting Thomas look my mother had given me. They said they'd give it a quick check and then I could probably go home. Legs akimbo once again, the nurse hooked me up to the little contraction monitor thing, did a double take, sort of came alive, and squawked: 'How did you not come earlier? You're in full labour! You need to go up to the delivery suite RIGHT NOW!' HA, in your face, Mum – I am Xena Bloody Warrior Princess. Only problem was I didn't have my hospital bag or carefully selected snacks or mags – but at least I had my mother's respect. Even though it would have been better to have had my own pillow. I knew that pain wasn't normal – and to this day, my mum trusts me a lot more when it comes to reporting how I am feeling. I just wish this had happened many years earlier and I could have had a whole load more days off of school.

Once in the delivery suite, the midwives just couldn't work out why my cervix was staying very much shut. I think every midwife on duty that night had a look up my nethers, until eventually a doctor was called and told us that the pessary hadn't unwound as it was supposed to. The translation being that the contractions were super intense but not long enough to actually move anything along – i.e. push the baby toward the emergency exit. It felt like someone was turning the key and the engine was revving but not igniting.

By this point it had been happening for a good eight hours and the pain was just getting worse and worse. So they put me on the gas and air. Now, I'd been to university, I'd been to Reading Festival – I knew how this stuff worked. Only gas and air works differently to a laughing gas balloon, let me tell you that before you do what I did. The hospital gas and air is continuous – it is an ENDLESS laughing gas balloon – and so within about a minute I was off my nut and what would be about six balloons deep. I was soon hallucinating that I was at a house party in Leeds and drifting in and out of consciousness, when suddenly . . . 'Fucking hell, it's CHRIS TARRANT!'

Now this was definitely unexpected. With my legs spread apart and a team of medical professionals potholing up my vagina on a rescue mission for the missing pessary, the host of *Who Wants to Be a Millionaire?* had appeared like a 'Where Are They Now?' mirage. I later discovered this was the female doctor who was about to perform the delicate retrieval operation. Chris Tarrant told me to breathe deeply and stay calm as she (or should I say he?) essentially fisted me and unravelled the curled-up pessary in one single motion, which I would liken to being waxed from the inside out. 'PHONE A FUCKING FRIEND!' I yelled. The room fell silent. The mission was complete. It was 9 p.m. at night.

With calm restored, I was soon plugged into an epidural and ready to get this show back on the road. But now I was a bit scared. That pessary was about the size of a slither of spaghetti, whereas babies were bigger – even bigger than Chris Tarrant's fist. Again, I wished I was a man. But epidural in, I could put my feet up – literally, I couldn't walk – and wait for things to kick in. Things kicked in until – joy – I couldn't even feel my ass any more.

My main midwife was called Marian and was there by my side throughout that night. As I ate lots of Boots BLT sandwiches, we talked about everything. We looked through my *heat* magazine and I told her about set-up pap shots and blew her mind. These being where celebrities tip off the paparazzi when they are going to be sunbathing and get a cut of the money and a look at the pictures before they get sent to the newspapers and magazines. 'Now whenever you see a picture of a celebrity on the beach, you will know why they've just had a blow dry and are wearing purple lipstick,' I told her. FYI, I stand by the theory that celebrities always have their hands up in the air 'enjoying the waves' and the like because it's the most slimming angle.

Marian said she hadn't been on holiday in the last two years since she started working nights.

So instead, we talked about women having babies and what percentage of them actually do a poo during the birth and I asked whether I would. Marian said no, I wouldn't.

Sometimes people lie not because they are dishonest but because they are kind. That's why I hate people who say 'I say what I think' as if this is a noble claim when, in fact, a lot of the time it just means you are rude. The reason we don't all go around saying 'what we think' all the time is to save people's feelings and make them feel safe. Marian told me I wasn't going to do a poo because she wanted me to feel safe. She was like the Irish mum in *Titanic* who reads the bedtime story to her children knowing they are imminently facing certain frozen watery death. So thank you, Marian. I did really believe I would just pop that baby out, and that the worst was over. That I wouldn't do the poo that I definitely did do.

Feeling like I was suspended from the actual world, it seemed beyond weird to be able to still check my phone and see what WhatsApp was saying. I was starting to think I wouldn't mind a few more nights in with Marian, nice and cosy with nothing but the sound of the little heartbeat machine thing to keep us company. Being now the dead of night, they'd dimmed the lights and as the room was the size of an airing cupboard it began to feel like we were nestled in our own little womb. We'd been up all night chewing the fat – it was like the best post-lash session of my life, only minus the random guy playing a guitar. But time goes fast when you can't feel your legs and before I knew it she was delivering the news:

'OK, it's time to push.'

Fuck.

OK, I need to buy more time. I need to buy more time to avoid having to actually give birth. Because giving birth isn't something I want to do, to be honest. Well, really, does anyone? Ideally, wouldn't we all prefer to just skip this part? Maybe if I asked really nicely they would agree to sedate me? Or failing that, maybe if I go really, really mental then they will sedate me anyway. How about just one more BLT? I've got loads of secrets about *OK!* magazine I could tell you.

Alas no, my time was up – it was time to get this baby out. The eagle had landed. The fat lady had sung. RIP vagina. The private doctor, the enabler of this induction, was then called to be at the front line. Have you ever got on a rollercoaster and it's only when your seat is locked in that you realise that there is no escape and that you actually really want to get off? That's, for me, what this moment felt like.

It was around this time Lorcan arrived with his news of the iPhone 6. 'OMG, have you heard the news? Apparently, people have been queuing around the corner at the Apple shop ALL NIGHT!' Er, sorry but that was NOT 'the news' for me that day – in fact at this point Freddy may well have stuck his hand out my vagina and said: 'Hey man, I'm the real news. And I've been stuck here waiting for this damn cervix to open ALL NIGHT.' Just as a reminder to Lorcan that we were busy frying somewhat bigger fish.

Now there were four of us in the airing cupboard an estate agent would definitely describe as 'bijou' and it had gone from cosy to cramped. So cramped that, over-excited as he was about the iPhone 6, Lorcan managed to gesticulate himself into the gas and air machine which launched off like that really intense bit in *Gravity*. Centimetres from my mother's face, Marian managed to grab it just in time and the unexpected intermission was over, buying me a good three minutes in which I didn't have to give birth. In an attempt to anchor down his hands, I armed Lorcan with a camcorder, just in time for the fun to really begin.

Whoever says 'pushing' isn't like doing a massive poo obviously hasn't ever had really bad constipation. They say push and you push like you haven't pushed since you were two years old straining on your potty. 'That's it, RIGHT into your bottom,' said Marian as she moved another paper towel from under my bum. Think Pizza Hut ice cream factory machine. Sorry, for those reading in Pizza Hut.

'YOU CAN DO IT, YOU CAN DO IT!' Lorcan said into my ear, and right into my ear – he was so close it sounded like he was saying it through a string and a tin can. In fact, everyone was very close due to the airing cupboard nature of the room, which seemed to be getting smaller and smaller with every push. With everyone's focus on me, giving birth was like putting on a show and it was up to me to give the audience what the ticket had promised. A BABY. Ever the entertainers, my internal organs certainly delivered a show after they decided to projectile vomit the earlier-eaten sandwiches during Every. Single. Push. Visually, it was all very *Little Britain*'s Maggie. If only puking were a competitive sport, I would have finally found my calling.

In an attempt to stall the BLT puke tsunami, my ever-resourceful birth partner Lorcan grabbed what was nearest and shoved it in my mouth. An XL maxi pad. My best friend tried to cork me with sanitary products. Having exhausted and over-flowed every sick bowl in the airing cupboard, he maintains to this day 'it was all that was left'. I grabbed it out my mouth and threw it back in his face, pushing him into the emergency call button like a clumsy Basil Fawlty juggling bowls of soup, or in this case sick. This prompted a conga line of the entire medical team on shift that morning to file in and line up for a look at the incredible spread-eagled vomiting woman. Realising that there was no medical emergency after all they conga-ed out as fast as they had come in.

After about eight pushes, in a torrent of regurgitated BLT sandwiches, it became apparent that I was crap at pushing.

Excellent at puking, though. 'We're going to need to give you a ventouse to help ease the baby out,' said Marian. 'What the fuck is a ventouse?' I thought. I didn't say it as I'd been rendered silent by the BLT vomit jet. Unbeknownst to me, they were going to hoover 'baby' out with essentially an oversized toilet plunger. They say ventouse to make you go along with it. Medical jargon, it is. Be smart, know the truth. And so more larger-than-ideal instruments entered my vagina to heave out the little womb lodger once and for all. And at 10:01 a.m. Freddy was hoovered into the world, not before giving me a second-degree tear on the way out. In that blaze of flailing sani-pads and an acute awareness I WAS doing a shit, I became a mum and I would never be alone again.

I'd watched enough *One Born Every Minute* to now expect a rush of unconditional love and a well-placed tear for the birth video footage. Suddenly I became two people. Two hearts. Two brains. Two souls and it became real – I'd made a person. A person like me who would have ups, downs, happy days, sad days. I'd made a person I was now responsible for. Could I do it? Could this person be happy? Am I worthy of him? Am I capable of having him? Am I worthy of his love, his unconditional love, his LIFE? Seeing the baby in the flesh, the responsibility of it all felt like it was engulfing me. I felt very out of my depth, intimidated by what I'd done and confronted with the possibility that I might not be a good mum. Making a baby doesn't instantly make you a good parent. What if I couldn't do it?

That's what I was thinking, but what did I say? 'WELL, THERE'S NO MISTAKING WHO HIS DAD IS!' I didn't need to say this, I didn't want to say this – but I did. This is the first thing I ever said in front of my perfect, seconds-old son and I'm ashamed – ashamed because his biology has never and will never play a part in any of my decision-making or my love for him.

And in front of everyone in that room, it was the first thing to trip off my tongue before I'd even touched my child. There's no defence for what I said but trying to explain it, even just to myself, I think the impact of nine months of people saying, 'You do KNOW, though, don't you?' had subconsciously taken its toll. I'd begun to feel like the paternity was something I needed to prove. And looking at my baby, who I swear had curled hair as he was born, I felt I had the proof in front of me. He looked enough like him. We spent hours afterwards trying to wipe it off the birth video but it remains – a document of my instantly regrettable words. And need for an eye test as Freddy definitely does NOT have curly hair.

All the while, more action was taking place down the business end. Well, after the party comes the after-party after all – in this case, in the form of afterbirth. So this is where you have to give birth AGAIN, as an encore of sorts. I looked around at the post-birth landscape to see literal blood on the walls. The tiny room looked like a scene from *Crime Scene Cleaners* or the morning after the most fucked-up house party of all time. BLT, bodily fluids and other things that should never be smeared together had even covered the gas and air machine. But before we had a moment to digest what had happened, in a gale of exit-bound placenta my baby was gone. I was so busy wallowing in my own internal drama, I didn't notice that the innocent in all this – the one who didn't ask to be involved –

had been taken away. As I was being stitched up for so long I expected to look down and see the Bayeux Tapestry, a new doctor, possibly one from the conga line, was standing in front of me. I knew he was a doctor because he was wearing his own shirt and tie. I'd seen enough 24 Hours in A&E to know that if you wore your own clothes, then you weren't small fry.

He said my baby had been taken to a place called Skoobu, I think he called it. There had been a problem with the birth. He explained fast and I struggled to take everything in.

'Your baby has a patch on his brain; as he was born he had a seizure and now he's in Skoobu,' he said.

I only later realised he was saying 'SCBU', the acronym for Special Care Baby Unit.

'What do you mean, a patch?' I asked.

'We're not sure yet,' he said.

'A dead patch?' I added.

'Possibly,' he replied.

'As in brain damage?' I was desperate now.

'Possibly.' His face showed no emotion.

The world stopped.

The other doctor was still on the front line of needlework. She didn't look up.

'Can I see him?' I asked.

'No, not yet,' I was told.

'But what is the problem?' my mum piped up.

'There's something wrong with his brain,' the doctor said plainly.

There was a silence. Then my mum asked: 'Will he lead a normal life?'

'We really can't say at this stage,' we were told. That answer stood out and we stopped asking any more questions.

Of course, we translated his neither yes or no as 'definitely not' – how many children with 'something wrong with their brain' do you know who lead 'normal lives'?

My mum left the room to be sick with shock. Lorcan just held on to me as I cried so hard that I lost my voice. He later said it was one of the most traumatic experiences of his life being in that room with me as we contemplated a future we had never even countered as a possibility. I felt like the world had stopped and my life was suspended in that room where the walls were still smeared with God knows what – like I was watching us from a bird's eye view.

Weirdly, or not considering my obsession with *heat* magazine, I thought about Katie and Harvey Price. I thought about how she managed this news as a single woman. How, despite what anyone says about her, she is so strong when it comes to her son. Whatever you might think about anything else she does, she cares for her disabled child fairly flawlessly. But I also thought about caring for an adult, or working out care for an adult when I became too old to do it myself. My mind went back and forth through every possible scenario, each more upsetting and surreal than the last.

After about an hour, finally someone came back into the room and told us: 'You can come and see your son now.' But I didn't want to – I didn't feel this child in this situation was MY son. I'd just come to terms with the idea of having a son in the first place, let alone a child with a disability. I felt guilty that I'd created this person whose life would be so difficult. I still couldn't walk because of my epidural so I was pushed in a wheelchair down to the special care rooms. As Lorcan pushed me I sobbed uncontrollably and couldn't imagine ever stopping or feeling normal ever again. We entered into a jungle of incubators as I braced myself for what I might see.

'Freddy Nickell' read the sign on the incubator and silently I peered in. He was far bigger than the other babies in the room and was a mish-mash of wires and plasters. He was wearing a tiny cap of wires and seeing this I said: 'My baby's brain doesn't work.' I thought saying it out loud might help it sink in. The nurse in the room overheard, walked over to us and pointed to the machine next to his incubator.

'Looks like it's working fine to me. Look!' The machine linked to the tiny cap of wires displayed an ongoing hum of activity.

It was a brain monitor.

'His brain is . . . normal?'

'As far as I can see – he probably just got a shock on the way out. Loads of babies end up on a drip just in case.'

'But they said . . .'

I drifted off and just looked at the machine and the baby. This big, 7 lb baby in a room of premature babies who really needed special care. I felt like I'd realised I was having a bad dream and finally managed to wake up. They'd made a mistake. There was no damage to his brain. I was later told that if it had been anything really serious he would have been taken to another department – NICU, the neonatal intensive care unit – so we could have known it wasn't life-threatening just from the fact he was taken where he was. Apparently, around one in eight babies are taken to SCBU after they are born.

It later emerged that Freddy had had a seizure when he was born and was hooked up to an antibiotic drip because there was a slight chance – a very slight chance – he had a brain infection. There was no damage to his brain, just a slight, teeny chance he had an infection. We'd simply been given the wrong information. But you believe what you are told; why would we have thought to ask for a second opinion? Especially as I'd just pushed a baby out.

By the time the hospital realised their mistake it was too late to take Freddy suddenly off the drip and so we both had to stay in the hospital for an extra five days. Two floors and about a hundred corridors separating us – which I would traipse every three hours to go and feed him. That night my friends Talia and Judith turned up at the hospital clutching Prosecco and chocolate. Having kept my pregnancy off social media, we staged our very own 'girls' night in' photoshoot cheersing the Prosecco while carefully cropping out any evidence we were in a hospital. I wore my glasses to cover up my swollen eyes. It probably looked like the most woeful pre-drinks of all time but it made me feel better. They'd both come from work and it seemed as if we'd spent the day on different planets. I tried to tell them what had happened but struggled to articulate just how awful an experience it had been. The hilariousness of the birth, the BLT vomit jet and Chris Tarrant seemed insignificant now – all I could remember was the aftermath and that hour thinking I was a mother to a disabled child. Talia said that she'd spoken to Lorcan on the phone afterwards and he'd been hysterical. He'd held it together for me but I think he suffered just as much as I did that day. Not that he ever let on – not even a bit.

That night I fell asleep for the first time as a mum but woke around 3 a.m. with a jolt, feeling an almost magnetic pull to go and see my baby. I didn't know why, but I just had to be near enough to touch him. I traipsed down the corridors and two flights of stairs to the special care unit and eventually got to his space. I still couldn't pick him up as he was hooked up to so many wires so I just put his tiny hand between my fingers until I felt him squeeze. He lay silent and peaceful with his arms in the air and his tiny fists clenched together, like a teeny sleeping Mexican wave. In that moment, I saw my future and it looked as peaceful and happy as he did.

All that nonsense about the fact he wasn't a girl – well, it was irrelevant. He could have come out a baby kangaroo and I would have worshipped him just the same. And those worries about football and rugby? For this little man, I'd convince Danny Cipriani himself to teach us the rules and train us personally. From the moment we met, Freddy gave me the sense that together we could do anything. I'd finally met my soulmate. I realised I could never have had any other baby but this baby.

It took three days from the birth to rule out any infection at all. For anyone put in the same situation, I now know that if it was anything as serious as we were led to believe he would have been taken to another hospital. Loads of children get taken to special care as a precaution – although previous to mine going I didn't even know it was a thing let alone a possibility. In my opinion women should be warned this beforehand by their midwifes. That hour gave me even more respect for parents who do have to deal with such realities without the change in the plot ending. But I have my theories about what really happened that morning. I truly believe that if I hadn't had the induction and if I'd left things to nature none of this would have happened.

If I am lucky enough to have another baby one day, I am 100 per cent hypnobirthing. It sounds like something straight from the Shangri-La field at Glastonbury but this is how someone explained it to me: 'You wouldn't force your body to do a poo when it wasn't ready, would you? But when you are ready and everything is in working order, it's easy.' It's less Goop and more common sense, when you come to think about it. My old boss was the one who first told me about it. Birth is a natural process and getting your body primed and ready to do everything for itself seems obvious to me now. I tried to fight against nature and take it into my own hands; perhaps if I hadn't, things could have been a little more straightforward. Trying to tug him out when we did – well, I imagine it was like a *Police Camera Action!* camera crew rocking up at my cervix. Even if it did make for some great anecdotes that Lorcan and I are still fond of whipping out when dinner parties get dull.

I decided to name him Frederick – Freddy to his friends. My mum lost her dad Frederick when she was thirty and had never stopped missing him. I had never met him but knowing how much he meant to my mum, I wanted to pay tribute to him by using his name. Although for one mad twenty minutes during labour, flying high on gas and air, he was momentarily called Eddie. But in sane land, it was always Frederick.

I also gave him two middle names – William, after my granddad and uncle, and Rupert, after my dad. I wasn't sure if I'd be having any more sons so I crammed all my tributes into one.

Frederick Rupert William Nickell was here. Now it was time to see what all the fuss was about.

# 5

# FALLING IN ALL THE LOVE

**B**efore I gave birth and did all that poo I'd only ever held one newborn baby. That was my nephew Charlie when I was fourteen and I remember promptly putting him down again because I had on those stick-on nails and was scared he would somehow ping them off. I didn't fancy holding another one after that. So when it came to holding Freddy for the first time once he was released from his incubator, I felt as unsteady as a child putting on a new pair of rollerskates. The nurses helped me but it still took a few attempts and a lot of nerves before I felt I'd got the knack. Well, those newborn heads are very flimsy, especially to a novice like I was.

There was a definite initial feeling of motherly incompetence. But incarcerated in Watford Hospital for five nights, we found ourselves in baby boot camp. It turned out that there was a silver lining to the brain damage incident. Unexpectedly, those Skoobu nurses taught me everything there was to know about caring for a newborn. They were patient, they were kind and that's why I bought them all heaps of posh chocolate when we were eventually released. Leaving your baby in the hands of strangers could be terrifying but they made it safe. Every nurse we encountered loved her job and took pride in making the time as easy as possible for the new mums. I felt like we were in it as a team and when we finally left it felt like a graduation of sorts. In return, I told them all my best secrets about the *X Factor* judges and bought them miniature bottles of Prosecco to take home after their shifts. Thank you, all the special care baby nurses – you made me ready to go home and be a mother and I don't know what I would have done without you.

In Scandinavia nowadays and in Britain in the 1970s, mums are and were kept in hospital after their babies are born to equip them for motherhood before they are sent packing. It's standard to expect such motherhood training. When I was in hospital I saw women leaving after a matter of a few hours. Lots of people who manage to not even stay a night in hospital are happy to be home so quickly but I know, for me, I needed that hands-on help. There's only so much you can teach expectant mums with a plastic doll or a diagram – having the nurses there with the actual baby was invaluable. They also cleared up the big, black poo that newborn babies infamously do right after they were born – in fact, I never even saw it. So it was worth that extra stay just to dodge that grotty bullet.

The only thing that I didn't appreciate in Skoobu was the labelling on Freddy's incubator. They were obviously standardised signs that didn't take into consideration that parental set-ups come in all shapes and sizes. Keeping to the nuclear norm, Freddy's name badge featured a lined space for his mum's name and next to that a lined space for his dad's. In the space left for Freddy's dad there was just a penned dash. The blank space set up our family as incomplete – I didn't realise then, but we weren't. But it perpetuated my feeling that I had short-changed my perfect son. That his life featured a gap that I couldn't fill, that he was missing something. That sign summed up the way I think society looks at single-parent families – that we have a vacancy. If this is the message we are sending out, is it any surprise that children from single-parent families can feel singled out (no pun intended)? A good mum is a happy mum – and having the feeling you aren't giving your baby a 'normal' family doesn't make you happy. Families come in all different permutations – what about the mummy and mummy or the daddy and daddy set-ups? It's surely commonsense that a mama who feels encouraged and celebrated will do a better job than one who feels judged. Every parent – married, single, man or rat – needs support instead of judgement, no matter what their circumstance.

But after five days, we ditched that sign and the incubator – we were finally free, liberated from Watford General Hospital. Watch out world, Freddy had arrived. There are few things weirder than realising you are walking out of a hospital as two people after arriving as one. Clutching the car seat, I felt like a nurse should be running after me for stealing. I was a person who more often than not avoided even carrying a purse. I'd rather just have my debit card loose in my bag, which is why I'd lost my debit card three times already that year. Now I had a baby bag with nappies, muslins, baby wipes, my own decanted breast milk, a car seat and oh, an actual baby. I couldn't just ring up a number and get that replaced if I lost it. What a difference nine months could make, eh? It was a Thursday. I know that because James O'Brien was doing 'Mystery Hour' on LBC. This was Freddy's first taste of the outside world and indeed, talk radio.

Arriving home, my mum surprised us with a huge zero balloon and loads of flowers and new baby cards. I felt so grateful, so accepted, so wonderfully lucky that I just burst into tears. Unlike the tears I cried at the start (middle and end) of my pregnancy – these weren't diluted half-happy, half-sad tears – these were just 100 per cent happy tears. I decided to see the zero as the start of my new life, and set against a backdrop of eating with one hand and shoving maxi sani pads down my (very large) pants, the next chapter started.

One of the first things we had to do, when Freddy was just ten days old, was register his birth. Sitting in the waiting area of Watford Registry Office, I thought *this* is what NCT classes would have been like, a heady cocktail of rusks, optimism and joy. And being here amid all this pesky happiness made me all the more relieved that I had decided to dodge them. The waiting area was just wall-to-wall solid couples. Solid couples accompanied by a tiny human-filled car seat. The happy new parent couples mixed in with a few couples there to register to get married. I wasn't sure which my mum would prefer me to be more. I willed my brain to blare out Destiny's Child 'Independent Woman' to remind myself it was OK to be here on my own. You don't actually have to take the baby to register a birth, just his hospital records – the 'red book' I would go on to forget at every appointment ever – so I thought Freddy would probably prefer to take his chances being left at home with his nanny.

This was the first time I had been away from him since he was born and although it had only been ten days it was already disorientating to be a whole car journey away from him. I switched between missing him loads to feeling like the whole thing hadn't happened, that I was just on my way to the train station to get back to London after a weekend at my parents.

I took my dad with me to the registry office under the guise of moral support. Really, I still couldn't fit my tits behind the steering wheel and the second-degree tear was still proving problematic. We were greeted by the registrar who was called Barbara. We asked her if she minded if we filmed the appointment for our birth video so we could show Freddy when he was older, or just when we got home seeing as he wasn't actually there. She agreed and suddenly morphed from normal Barbara to how I imagine Barbara would be if she did amateur dramatics.

'Firstly, congratulations!' she said really very enthusiastically indeed as we sat down in the office. I'm going to like this Barbara, I thought to myself. We put the video camera on the table and I noticed her eyes kept darting to it every few seconds like it was her Andy Warhol five minutes of fame. I bet she's great when she does weddings, I thought, making a mental note to book her if I ever did get hitched.

'And what do YOU do?' she asked. No, this wasn't small talk – the mother's profession needs to be added to the birth certificate. And the father's, in the cases that there is one.

'I'm a journalist, actually,' I replied.

'Oh right, would I have seen you in anything?' she said.

Well, unless Barbara was familiar with the Yahoo homepage, it was unlikely. And no one was familiar with the Yahoo homepage. Not even people with Yahoo email addresses.

'Um, no I doubt it,' I said.

The only person to ever have recognised me from anything was the cashier in the Marble Arch McDonald's who asked for my autograph. I was so shocked I asked him for a photo as a memento of the moment. I also took a picture of the 'autograph'. I told Barbara this story but could tell she was disappointed so I tried to placate her with an anecdote about who the most unfriendly member of Little Mix is. She looked suitably appeased, just in time for the part where you have to declare the father.

'So that's Mum's details done, and now on to Dad!' she said. As she spoke she started to smile and gesture to my 61-year-old dad who, no offence to him, doesn't look any younger.

'Er, he's MY dad,' I said.

Stumbling for a quick response, Barbara laughed, 'Ah I see! Well . . . stranger things have happened.' My dad looked weirdly proud of his momentary imagined fertility, only managing to snap out of it to chip in: 'Yeah, she had the baby but she forgot the husband part! HAR HAR HAR.' Cheers, Dad. Barbara looked as awkward as I felt and took a nervous glance into the lens of the video camera which I had set up on the table. Er, did Barbara just wink?

Apparently age-gap incest seemed more likely than it being just me on my own on the birth certificate. But it was just me and the paternal side was just left a big ol' blank space. On the certificate it reads, 'Mother: Amy Nickell. Father: unknown.'

Well, selectively unknown – because I sure knew who he was and somewhere he knew who he was. I suddenly wondered where he was right in that moment. I'd do this a lot during the first few days of motherhood – drift off and wonder if we'd crossed his mind.

It felt necessary to divulge the whole story to the now bewildered Barbara who thought I'd just had a baby with my dad. I think after she realised my dad wasn't the father she then wanted it to be a celebrity love child. No such luck. But she got the full conception story from Yahoo Christmas party to eventual abandonment. Well, I didn't want her to think I just didn't know and couldn't keep track of my personal sperm transactions, celebrity or otherwise. I ended up gabbing on so much that I lactated through my silky top. The whole cringeworthy spectacle is captured forever on my video camera.

Later that day, my grandad came to meet Freddy and we had a picture taken of the four generations together. If you look close enough you can see a tiny little milk stain on my top – a mark of my endless gabbing. But rather than even mention or question where this surprise baby originated from, my grandad just loved him. And I loved my grandad more than ever for that. Even though my mum maintains that he thought I had a husband who worked on oil rigs and would be back in six months. It wasn't an everyday occurrence for my grandad to visit; normally I only saw him at Christmas if I was lucky. Well, life just gets in the way, doesn't it? That's what I told myself to feel less bad about being a lazy granddaughter. It also didn't help that every time he came to visit I would have to put special stage make-up over my tattoo under my mother's instructions.

In fact Freddy served as the perfect excuse to reconnect with friends and family I hadn't seen for ages. Finally I saw all those friends to whom I'd been saying 'We need to catch up!' and really meaning it but somehow not managing it for months. I think everyone I regarded as a real friend made the pilgrimage to Berkhamsted to meet the little prince within the first month he was born. They came bearing gifts but it was my friend Judith who trumped the lot when she came bearing Nando's.

If you ever feel at a social loss, have a baby. I've never had so many friends and family swarm round me in the weeks following Freddy's birth. It was like a revolving door of old friends, delightfully crawling out the woodwork to come and meet the newest member of the family. I've long loved a long-winded handwritten message in a card and my new baby cards brought out the full-on Tolstoy in almost everyone. It was really, well, lovely and ever since I always try and think of something special to say in cards because it just gives them so much more oomph.

Freddy, being only a few weeks fresh to the world, stayed pretty underwhelmed for his first meetings, unaware he was getting more social interaction than most people get in years. Of course, it was only a matter of time before we set him up with his own Facebook account to keep his aunties and uncles in the loop with daily photo updates.

Some friends I hadn't seen in so long, I had to unleash the whole conception circumstances to them. It was different telling people with the baby in my arms compared to before. With the baby present, the judgment disappears – no one put their two pence in, no one mentioned the 'a' word that rhymes with shcmabortion. Well, not out loud anyway. In my head, single mums still required explanation though. So as well as with friends, I felt the need to justify my situation to strangers a lot in those early days. Freddy had to go for a hearing test and all the lady in the waiting room heard was my tale of abandonment. She had her own free hearing test that day and I bet she'd have very much preferred to have been deaf.

'It was HIS decision, not mine,' I'd tell anyone who'd listen. Sometimes I considered telling them that I had a dead husband – taking any potential blame off me. I felt then like I needed to explain our family. It was Radio Abandonment and anyone who even looked at us would receive a verbal load. I've since realised our family is something to celebrate rather than explain. If even my own grandad didn't need an explanation then neither did anyone else. Even though I knew by then that I wouldn't change a thing. Except my milky top, that is.

When I was pregnant, everyone told me: 'It'll be tough once he's here, but so worth it when you look at his little face.' I had no idea what they were talking about. From what I'd heard, all babies did was wake you up all night, shrink your tits and shit a lot. How could a snotty little mug make that lot fly? 'Yeah, we'll see about that,' I thought. Yet, about two days in, after a lot less sleep and new but not improved boobs – somehow, it was definitely all worth it. And all I had to do to know was look at that little face. Call it a miracle of nature, but I was smitten. Once it all sunk in it was like a switch flipped. I have never felt happier or happiness like I did the week after Freddy was born. I had fallen hook, line and sinker in total love with my home-grown human. I knew he'd be cute in an Andrex puppy kind of way but this was next-level stuff.

It's like taking all the love you have ever felt in your life and then doubling it. Hell, tripling it ten million times. I think I'd just been practising being happy up until now. Before was just the rehearsal and this was the real deal. It was the ultimate high. And like I said before, I'd been to Reading Festival and university, now I'd even GIVEN BIRTH – the ultimate trip – so I had perhaps once or twice felt a share of other highs. And some of those really did feel euphoric, if artificially so. But this was next level. With no comedown to speak of. A hundred per cent totally natural, purely brain-made euphoria and it was awesome. Bonding hormones are the new MDMA, you heard it here first. Plus, unlike when I tried MDMA, I didn't have to drive for two hours cross-country to have a cuddle from my mum and bake a gingerbread house the day afterwards. To this day, my mum still thinks I was just really, really homesick. I remember I was latching Freddy on for a night feed during one of our nights in Skoobu when I realised what these feelings reminded me of. I told the nurse on shift that night the only other time I have ever felt something similar without the aid of chemical enhancement was when I became infatuated with Colin, the ice rink marshall, my first ever boyfriend when I was fourteen.

I remember vividly being so obsessed with him and his speed skates and snogging which was akin to a tongue thumb war that I couldn't physically fall asleep and staying up all night willing my imagination to calm down so I could get some rest. But there would be no rest for the wicked and I couldn't and I was very tired for school the next day. As soon as Freddy was born, I couldn't fall asleep easily. My brain was just buzzing about my new mini pal. New mums complain that they don't have much sleep – but I didn't want to sleep, I wanted to gawp at my baby and grin. 'I just hope he loves me even one tenth of how much I love him,' I prayed. I looked forward to night feeds because they meant I would be able to wake him up. Sadly, just like my feelings for Colin, that didn't last forever. Soon I was knackered, just like BabyCentre had warned me. But the happy feeling did last. He was and is the best part of my day. All the clichés were true – when I saw him in the morning my heart literally rushed. I felt like that Doctor Seuss quote: 'You know you're in love when you can't fall asleep because reality is finally better than your dreams.'

'Screw boyfriends, my baby is definitely "the one",' I thought. And I thought this despite regular frankly unlovable acts which ordinarily would have been a total buzzkill coming from anyone else:

1. Projectile vomiting during my brother Martin's birthday meal . . . at my brother.

2. 1 a.m., 3 a.m., 6 a.m. and 9 a.m. milk demands.

3. Prompting an emergency stop over at South Mimms service station after an unstoppable milk demand went nuclear.

If a man did those things to me, I would definitely dump him. Before suggesting he visit his GP.

However, Freddy could do what he wanted and I just fell more in love with him. I actually looked up exactly what it was that was flooding my brain and making me feel so very excellent and it's a hormone called oxytocin. Someone needs to bottle this mother-baby bond stuff, I thought, because it's blimmin' incredible. I quickly discovered that someone already has after a late-night Google led me to a prescription-only oxytocin nasal spray. I didn't buy the nasal spray. OK, I did but I got too scared to try it so it's still in a drawer somewhere. But as the initial feelings settled, they just made way for the real deep love that only comes after infatuation. It all sounds a bit Mafia but I really would die for this person. I'm absolutely not perfect but when I made that little boy, I did something right. Gosh, that sounds wankerish, doesn't it? I wondered how I could have ever doubted that this was my correct path, that he wasn't so obviously a gift. Dramatic, yes, but true. And it's about to get even worse . . . I'm not religious but even I would catch myself believing in fate when I looked into his tiny little trusting eyes. SOMEONE PASS THE ANTI-NAUSEA TABLETS. Does my baby's head hurt? Because I swear he just fell from heaven. OK, you get it.

I sometimes think that these feelings were this intense because I had expected so little. I once read that happiness depends not on how well things are going but whether things are going better or worse than expected. And for me, things were definitely better than I expected. I only ever felt this independently so never missed having someone to share it with and to be honest, I'm happy I had this all to myself. I never liked sharing my toys when I was little either. Plus I had never really, to be honest, liked being part of a team, despite my CV saying otherwise. Mine and Freddy's bond was unbreakable from the off because it was only ever between us. And surprising as it was, this was the very thing that made it so special – it was us against the world in those early days.

My mum says Freddy looked like a 'wrinkled raisin man' when he was born but I just saw the most beautiful human perfection. I think, well I know, a mother's brain is hardwired to see her baby as beautiful – I now totally understand the saying 'a face only a mother could love'. Experiencing it first-hand, however, you don't realise how warped your perceptions are at the time – you honestly think your baby is abnormally genetically perfect. It's only looking back at the birth photos that you realise that he did, indeed, look like a wrinkled raisin man (soz, Fred, you're gorj now, by the way). That's why ALL parents secretly think their baby could make millions from baby modelling. We've all got maternal love goggles on. Apparently, just the smell of your baby triggers a physiological response in mothers similar to that experienced by hungry people presented with a delicious meal.

Motherhood also unleashed a protective streak in me that I never realised I had before. I became acutely aware that I would literally kill for this person. Well, try to anyway. 'Maternal aggression' it's called, apparently. Rife in the animal kingdom, according to my research. Touch wood, I am yet to have to put this to the test. But I'm sure two hours of Body Combat a week pretty much makes me a human weapon so y'all better watch out. And if you hurt my boy, I will unleash more than just a running man and a ropey left hook. And if it turns out I don't . . . then I will just have to outsource the violence to someone a bit harder. Because the thought of anyone making Freddy sad or harmed in any way definitely engages an inner mama bear who has just had her honey stolen. I read that last bit on an inspirational Pinterest quote.

But unconditional love and a hardwiring to kill didn't quite equate to an instant parenting ability. And there was so much still to learn in those early days, despite the wisdom imparted by the Skoobu nurses. At times I struggled but overall I never found it as 'tough' as I expected. Probably because I expected the very, very worst thing. 'Tough' is gruelling, 'tough' sounds like something you'd rather not be doing – facing a huge mound of washing up is 'tough', hoovering is 'tough'. I now know TOD-DLERS are TOUGH. For me, looking after a newborn baby all cosy in my house was not tough. Maybe I just got lucky because Freddy was a pretty predictable baby – it was always obvious what he wanted and he was easily soothed. Plus, I'd totally nap when he did. I didn't have a household to run, another child to look after or really, anything else to worry about, so I was far from the state of exhaustion other mums feel. Even if I was doing every single feed myself, no negotiation possible. And night feeding was the price to pay, delivered to new mums by the devil, for all that delicious oxytocin-fuelled love and cosy loveliness.

The Dalai Lama once said, 'sleep is the best meditation'. Human alarm clocks going off every three hours are not. These were the only times in my baby son's new life that I ever wished I were in a partnership – just to share the relentless three-hourly, two-hourly or just plain hourly wakings. There's no certainty in night feeding, no beginning or end – your sentence is unknown. With this in mind, a fully charged iPhone, Netflix subscription and a good snack selection were essential.

During my night-feeding sentence, I managed to revisit old series I hadn't seen for years. Well, when I wasn't watching ITV's *Nightscreen* wishing I was the presenter spinning the wheel. I watched all twelve series of *Peep Show*. Mark's baby took on a whole new dimension. There is a bit where Sophie is giving birth and he freaks out and goes to KFC and an arcade and I totally knew how he felt. I also rewatched all the episodes of *Friends* where Rachel has the baby. Again, I saw it through new eyes. Rachel was a single mum, Phoebe was a surrogate and Monica had to deal with infertility. In those dark hours with a baby on the boob, smothered in darkness and balls deep in my Netflix account, I started to realise that there is more than one way to be a parent. Whether there's one or two of you isn't what makes great parenting. There are rubbish single mums, there are rubbish married mums – your ability as a parent is not defined by your marital status. And if you are a single mama, rewatch all the episodes where Rachel becomes a mother – it's awfully comforting. Freddy, meanwhile, just laid back and guzzled milk in between making windy faces that I would tell everyone were smiles.

But caring for that days-old squidge wasn't always as straightforward as a boob in the gob and a flick of the remote control. With feeding, comes winding. And winding quickly became the bane of my life and something I was certainly not forewarned about. Why does changing nappies get such bad press when winding exists as a thing in the world? 'It's just burping a baby ffs, you bloody amateur,' you might think. But it wasn't. Or at least in Freddy's case, it definitely wasn't. And if you don't manage to get that trapped air out then say hello to certain indefinite screaming – definitely enough to interrupt my early-hours telly sessions. I admire any soul who masters the art of early-days winding. I also would like to pay tribute here to the makers of Infacol, which fast became known as 'the saviour' in our house. For those who aren't in the know, it's basically Rennie for babies, eliminating those pesky bubbles before they have time to interrupt the *Peep Show* series six finale.

Infacol was a discovery made after a winding session fell onto stony ground, late one evening. I was having the type of sesh where whatever I did I couldn't stem the wailing. The type of sesh that leaves you convinced newborn babies should be used in interrogation rooms. It was probably about 11 p.m. – my mum was still up but was about to go to bed. I just couldn't, whatever I did, get the wind out of Freddy who was quickly going puce from all the screaming. I was imagining he had the kind of trapped wind you get after twelve hours in economy and so I was doing everything I could to push it out. I did the bicycle legs thing taught to me by the Skoobu nurses – no joy. I patted him from every angle possible. Backwards, frontwards – rubbing, pushing – harder, softer . . . still, nothing. It was like giving a drunk man a hand job.

My mum kept shouting 'GRIPE WATER' but Google was telling me he was too young. However, BabyCentre forums were all banging on about something called 'Infacol'. I decided it was worth a punt and embarked on a late-night mission to the local twenty-four-hour Tesco – the only place open with a pharmacy. There, in the baby aisle, amongst other grey-faced, pyjama-bottom-wearing new parents on emergency assignments, I noticed there was just one bottle left on the shelf – which I took as a sign it was good shit. Back home, I managed to cram some into his gummy mouth and the puceness gradually subsided. Peace was restored. It was a miracle. Infacol swooped in a number of other times when the struggle was real and I can't thank that magic stuff any more. Absolute game changer.

Strangely, I actually sought solace in nappy changing. Which was handy considering I was doing it ten times a day, which was coincidentally the same number of times a day I'd get asked, 'Is he sleeping through the night yet?' NO, HE'S TEN DAYS OLD YOU LUNATIC. There was a comforting certainty in nappy changing, a definite start and an end. With nappy changing, you know where you are. It was just like changing a miniature sanitary towel.

Prior to Freddy's arrival on earth, I had made plans to have a strict 'routine'. When I was pregnant I bought a Gina Ford book and I even wrote down timings on an Excel spreadsheet. However, that Excel spreadsheet quickly went out the window and I learned that babies dictate their own routine. It was far easier to take his lead. I'd let him wake up by himself and feed him totally on demand – and boy, did he take advantage of that little in-house perk.

During these long nights being an on-call cow, Facebook would keep me updated with the goings-on from my former world. It was the same old merry-go-round of interviews, free drinks and selfies with Z-listers but only I had stepped off. Not that anyone seemed to be noticing. Somehow the showbiz world kept turning without me. And that could make me feel very, very small. I could feel invisible. But then, in my cosy and calm newborn baby bliss, being used as a human udder, I honestly didn't mind. It could wait.

As I fell in love with Freddy, I also started to fall back in love with myself. Although I'd rarely admit it, I'd been hurt.

Frame it however you like, but I had been rejected and now I had to psychologically heal. I'd been ignoring it, insisting I was fine. But I'd been dumped as hard as a woman can be. 'Barry disliked me so much, he was willing to disown his own child,' I would catch myself thinking. I now accept that he was immature and terrified but then I just blamed myself and I was convinced Freddy would blame me too. Looking back, that time was an all-encompassing, gut-wrenching, soul-draining experience that I never anticipated having to go through. So when I eventually gave birth and stepped off the rollercoaster, I was mentally exhausted. Somehow Freddy served as an emotional first-aid kit for all that.

Moving home could have been a nightmare but taking myself away from London, away from my job and my friends was like time off. Time off I could use to reflect on where I'd been, emotionally and psychologically. I focused on the strength I had mustered to get myself to where I was now. I had a tiny tattoo of a triangle on my wrist as a reminder of my journey.

My pregnancy felt like a constant gamble and I'd put all my money on one single bet. But now, I found comfort in my baby. Freddy made something in my mind click; he just slotted in like my missing puzzle piece. The bet had paid off.

# 6

# SINGLE MUM MYTHS BUSTED

I f you'd asked me what a single mother looked like when I was twenty-two with my head hanging out the window in Golders Green, I would have probably described an image of a teenager with her hair scraped back, wheeling a buggy round Tesco in her pyjamas. I was unable and unwilling to understand anything other than that, because well, why would I? Single motherhood was very much not on my radar back then.

Never in four squillion, trillion light years would I have put myself in those pyjamas. Abandonment and mothering a bastard (soz, Fred) was not on the cards. I had no first-hand experience of single-parent families, my own parents having done things the traditional way by getting married and having me in that order. That 'normality' was all I knew; pretty much all of my information about what a single mum was like was derived from *Little Britain* and the *Daily Mail*, so yes, it was rather narrow. My mum had actually been a single mum herself after divorcing my older brothers' dad but she never mentioned it and my father was always considered their father for as long as I could remember. It was a part of her life that, then, I didn't ask questions about – we just accepted that my dad was theirs and that was it.

It's no wonder then really that when I found myself unexpectedly expecting, I was absolutely bloody terrified of my pregnancy, which in my eyes was obviously a one-way ticket to poverty and misery via a short stop-off at shame. On the plus side, single parenthood would mean a windfall of free cash off the government, right? Yeah, Freddy and I were going to have so much cash we could chuck it up in the air and make it rain like Jennifer Lopez in the bling-filled P Diddy 'Hey, look! I'm on a yacht!' era. But somehow we were also going to be so poor that I would have to work three jobs just to put a loaf of bread on the table à la that Clean Bandit 'Rockabye' song.

The rhetoric of the nineties and noughties, my 'formative' years, was hell-bent on badmouthing and just being, well, really damn shady to single mums, blaming them for all sorts of society's ills, something to rage about and be suspicious of. Basically, before the headlines came for the immigrants, they came for the single mums. In 1993 the Tory Social Security Secretary, Peter Lilley, matched the general vibe of the time when he labelled single mums as 'benefits-driven' and 'undeserving'. Thank goodness he didn't have an empty womb up for grabs, eh? He made no mention of the absent fathers, in case you were wondering. No one ever mentions the absent fathers. Twenty-odd years later and it's still the case; they tend to disappear in the narrative of the single mum.

I remember the only conversation I had heard growing up about single mums was when I was about ten and on holiday with my parents. It would have been 2000ish; I was all about Steps and Tinkerbell peel-off nail varnish and whether the millennium bug was really going to bring the nation to its knees. My parents made 'holiday friends' and were swapping gossip about their lives at home. The new holiday friend, let's call her Carol, was telling them the most scandalous story about an ex-girlfriend of her son. Carol reckons that after being dumped by her son and subsequently evicted from his flat, this girl had had a bright idea.

'Well, then she went and got knocked up, didn't she? We're still not sure by who, the sl—'

She then said a word beginning with 's' that I hadn't heard before.

My ten-year-old brain had no idea what link she was making.

'For the free council flat! You get pregnant – they just give them away,' Carol added.

Cue lots of outrage and talk of 'sponges' and 'taxpayers money' and my prejudices were set up for life. You do shame your family and get called a sponge and other words I hadn't heard before that also began with 's', but on the plus side, you get a free house. I imagined the type of house I'd seen on *My Super Sweet 16*. To be honest it sounded like this girl had her head screwed on to me; I didn't know what they were all getting so angry about. Little did anyone round that table realise that one day I'd be the 's'-word girl. Only I'm still waiting for my free flat.

But despite this cushty-sounding existence, MY main sex

education was to be repeatedly told 'do not get pregnant', and finding yourself unexpectedly expecting was the worst thing 'a girl like me' could possibly do. I'd most likely fare better walking into moving traffic than get accidentally up the duff. Early motherhood in general, not to mention flying solo, meant career suicide, getting fat, saggy boobs, depression, poverty, exhaustion, and the end of romance, sleep and all joy forever and a day. To be a single mother was to be a failure, dependent on handouts, a poster girl for 'Benefits Britain'. Vicky Pollard incarnate.

My mum had grown up in a world where if girls got accidentally pregnant they would most likely be packed off to mother and baby homes – or worse still, forced to give their babies up for adoption. She knew two girls that this actually happened to. She was born in 1946 so it would have been around 1966 that single parenthood was still seen as the ultimate sin. In the postwar world women who got pregnant out of wedlock – even in circumstances of rape – were considered little better than prostitutes. Many mother and baby homes would accept fees from adoptive parents, giving them the perfect motivation to actively encourage women to give up their children. Shockingly, twins were often split up to make sure two donations were received over one. Even more shockingly, some of these 'homes' were open until 1990. Often the mothers would nurse their babies for six weeks and then have them taken away, a pain no woman should have to suffer. When the mothers did stay at home, some families would cover up the pregnancy to avoid the public shame. Eric Clapton – yep, as in 'Layla' – grew up thinking that the woman who was actually his mother was his elder sister. If my own mum can remember this happening then you can't argue that it was long enough ago to not still have a hangover, to still be resonating in today's thinking.

As recently as 2007, David Cameron described unmarried mothers as a key sign of a 'broken society'. Ta, Dave. Good thing that pig got the morning-after pill, eh? The real thing that will break our society is attitudes like that. I've learned to never, ever judge. It was the fear of being judged that meant most girls in history rarely felt free to consider keeping and raising their babies. They felt they had no choice. Since 1948, unmarried mothers had been offered the same state support – albeit meagre – as widows to raise their children. This could be seen as evidence it was the stigma over the support that ruled the feelings that they didn't have a choice. But now, we do have a choice and we can explore our options. And we are doing just that and the last thing we need is archaic judgement that should stay put in the history books.

To my shame, I used to think how ridiculously stupid girls who got pregnant must be, and sometimes would come to the conclusion they must have done it on purpose. I was definitely a product of my single mum-bashing environment. Is it really any wonder some of this drivel managed to sneak in and set my internal agenda? I know the myths about single parenthood inside out because, well, I used to believe most of them. And that's why when I was pregnant and Freddy was born, I felt guilt. I felt guilt for depriving him of a dad, despite this being way beyond the realms of my control.

This is not the 1960s though; single parents are not excluded from 'polite society' like they used to be, but the negative opinions are still there, only the shade is more subtle this time round. There is still an assumption that single parents must be at a disadvantage for facing parenthood alone. That they stay in, funded by the state and suffocated by motherhood and shitty nappies, while their social and employment opportunities fade away in the time it takes to get the *PAW Patrol* theme tune stuck in your head. I know that when I gave birth I was only given leaflets on what benefits I was entitled to rather than any information on going back to work or education.

As sure as day turns to night, so the myth of the undeservedly rich and pathetically poor single mother continues. Single mothers used to be seen as the dregs of society, dually sponging away at both the welfare system and our poor old exes, who now live in disaster relief tents while we watch Mr Tumble on our diamond-encrusted flat screen and don't go to work. Nowadays single mums are more often seen as pitiable figures scraping by in some godforsaken tower block and feeding their children on food bank donations.

The reality is pretty obvious really: when it comes to cash, some got it, some don't. Personally, I don't take any money from my Freddy's biological dad. Mainly because he's never offered but that's another story . . . Of course, every so often I indulge in the unhealthy (but totally satisfying) fantasy where I pawn everything he owns and leave him in that aforementioned disaster relief tent shivering in his underpants, after which I also sell said underpants, and the tent. But that's a story for another chapter and probably also a qualified therapist.

I haven't asked him to pay a penny, out of principle; I don't want him suddenly being able to say he has any stake in Freddy's life and future. I also don't just eat Aldi spaghetti hoops. I do shop in Aldi, but only because you'd be a fool not to – you haven't lived until you've sampled the Aldi random aisle. And yes, I do receive help from the government. But it's definitely not as much as you think, regardless of what newspaper you read. This is despite everything being geared toward two incomes – which perhaps explains the price of childcare. And Kidzania. And I have been paying tax for quite a while now, so please don't be too upset. I now rent privately and have never qualified for council housing despite being a single mum. I lived with my parents after having Freddy with one of the reasons being that financially, I don't know how I would have managed otherwise. I'm lucky; I realise that this isn't an option for everyone. So no, no free house to speak of. The reality of signing up for council accommodation in London may be years on the housing list, extended periods in 'temporary' accommodation, and potentially being moved miles away from your entire family/support network. So not exactly the red carpet rolled out that Carol imagined, eh? And as for teenagers getting pregnant to get a house? Less than 2 per cent of single parents are teenagers. The average age of a single mum is, in fact, thirty-eight.

Take every household bill and double it; that's what single parents deal with. That's why we need the tax credits and free childcare, because without them, on one income, things can get tricky. In fact, looking at any statistics it's financial stress and poverty that seem to be the real link to rates of depression, loneliness and kids' educational attainment. Before tax credits were introduced, so many more single parents were out of work. Now, the number of single parents in work equates to the same number of childless women in work for the first time. Which, when you think about it, is a statistic worth taking a LOT more notice of!

Just recently, the tide has turned and the 'poor' version of the single mum stereotype seems to have gained the upper hand. The new picture popularised in the press is the 'struggling single mum', which always makes me think of a big gaggle of us all in hiking gear half way up Ben Nevis. She can currently be seen grimacing on the front cover of celebrity magazines having just been deserted by her latest boyfriend, and appearing as a guest on the ITV morning show that rhymes with Leremy Bile.

She would also do anything to 'find love again', providing a convenient segue into my next single mum myth: that all we want is a replacement father. There is a rather pesky assumption that single mums must view their family as incomplete, and that we're therefore desperate to find a 'father figure' to fill the man-shaped hole in our life. 'You'll find someone,' smug-faced friends tell me, while potential new boyfriends freak out, convinced that one day I'll be handing them over to my son to explain what a wet dream is. But honestly, we are quite all right, thank you. I know it's a struggle to believe, but my existing relationships ARE enough. I don't need to look for anything because nothing is actually missing. Our family might not be traditional but it's also not incomplete – so stick that on a slogan T-shirt with my name on.

We might be a family of two, but we really aren't lonely. Becoming a single mum doesn't suddenly make you Tom Hanks in *Castaway* (Freddy playing the part of Wilson the football in this analogy). My 'lonely' levels are similar to those of any other singleton – so if you're doing the single thing right and aligning yourself with great friends and supportive family, they won't reach critical. Indeed, I recently read a statistic that single people have more individual social connections than married people because they don't put all their eggs in that one wedded basket. That's not to say we wouldn't want to open up our family to new members, but we're just as happy as a family of two as we would be three (or four? Or FIVE? Yikes).

Being a single mother is often still seen as going hand-in-hand with depression. But the link is understandable: with the inaccurate rep we've got, it's inevitable it will create a self-fulfilling prophecy for some of us. I think I'm even better off than the regular single folk, because how can I possibly be lonely after producing my very own pint-size sidekick? I mean, I can't even remember the last time I went to the toilet on my own. I rest my case. It takes a village to raise a child, not a mum and dad. And our village is currently so full it's one in one out. Child-rearing was apparently very different about five hundred years ago when the whole 'it takes a village' thing came about because it LITERALLY required a village. A child was nurtured by parents, grandparents, aunts, uncles and close families and that was just how we parented and raised our young. With time and modernisation, the 'village' shrank to just the two parents. That doesn't mean I'm not giving Tinder a few swipes when Freddy's in the bath. Mama still needs a snog every now and then, more of which in Chapter 9 (go on; skip straight to the juicy bits).

Which leads me to another single mum myth – we're promiscuous. I remember before I had Freddy, a male acquaintance told me that he preferred dating single mums for 'an easy lay'. Generalisation, much? Also, if we are – what's that to do with anyone? Now take your slut-shaming elsewhere, thanks. However, I understand if you have your concerns as to where I might be getting my snogs other than Tinder. I've heard WAY too many people (normally on the TV) say that some 'coupled-up mums' view us desperado single mums as predatory. Because a bit of casual adultery is exactly the kind of thing that would make our already complicated lives better ... Er, no thank you. Fear not, married mums, your middle-aged men are safe with you.

To be honest, I have never actually encountered this scenario in real life. I think it's more one that the early-morning TV shows and soaps like to push. On the contrary, sometimes I feel like my real life 'married mum' cohort are instead a bit jealous of my single status, which means that I don't have to collaborate when it comes to parenting decisions, I got to name my kid whatever the heck I wanted and didn't feel obliged to have sex after pushing 7 lbs of human out my love hole FOR A WHOLE YEAR. Every cloud and all that.

From experience, I now know everything I believed and feared was a load of rubbish. But I also know that sadly a good chunk of the population still think the way I used to. Knowing that Freddy is growing up in a world where this mind-set continues to go round and round makes me worry. That does make me feel guilty. That does make me want to grab a megaphone and read this chapter aloud to anyone who says otherwise.

People also seem rather shocked when you continue to have a life after you've had a baby. The general rhetoric is that Project Life ends when Project Baby begins. This just isn't true. The months I spent convinced I'd never do, well, anything ever again. Well, shock horror – it never came true. You can do exactly the same – just not as often and you might have to pay a babysitter and really miss your kid the whole time you are away. But here's a bombshell: last year I even went to Secret Garden Party for the weekend.

There were no single parent role models for me around when I was expecting. However, I've since discovered my own. If I'd had this lot to reference when I was pregnant I think I would have been so much more positive. Because looking at these women, I can't see one who sacrificed life for motherhood. Somehow, the two have managed to coincide.

### 1. *Joanna Lumley*

Joanna is the world's most glamorous single mum and basically my absolutely fabulous mumspiration. Having a baby at twenty-one didn't stop her becoming a model, actress and all-round superstar.

### 2. *Charlize Theron*

My pal (not) Charlize admits she 'never dreamed' of becoming a single mum but, like I found out, sometimes fate has other ideas. Confident in doing it on her own, she adopted her son Jackson from South Africa in March 2012.

### 3. *Sandra Bullock*

After divorcing her ratbag ex Jesse James, Sandra realised she didn't need a man to be the best mum to her adopted son totally on her own. She says she wouldn't say no to a relationship but that her family isn't missing a thing just because it's just the two of them. AMEN, SANDRA.

### 4. *January Jones*

January Jones has never spoken about the identity of her baby's dad and why should she? Knowing she was going to go through her pregnancy alone, she says she was excited and her child would be 'better off without a father'. She's now a proud mama to a son named Xander.

### 5. *Elen Rivas*

Ex-wife of footballer Frank Lampard, Elen Rivas summed up being a single mum to her two daughters when she said the important thing is to surround yourself with loved ones and friends you can trust. Basically, throw love and support at it and you can't go wrong.

### 6. *Jourdan Dunn*

Jourdan Dunn was a single mum to her son Riley, now four, when she was discovered as a model. Jourdan is catwalking proof that your career doesn't end the minute your waters break. In fact, the best could still be yet to come. Only now you get to share your success (and pay slips) with your miniature best mate.

This lot prove that anything is still possible and that giving birth is just a comma rather than a full stop in the sentence of your life.

Yet despite this list of success stories, every time I write about my experiences of single parenthood in a newspaper, my inbox is clogged by uninvited, aggressive messages, usually from men, prompting me to look at 'empirical evidence' that children from single-parent families are worse off than those living with both parents. I often wonder if these people would pass on the same judgement and information to a bereaved family left with only one parent? These comments aren't helpful, they won't change anything and all they do is prove people still have their beef with single mums.

Thanks to talk like this, I really believed I'd brought my baby into the world on a back foot. In our cultural fantasies, a team of two will always be number one when it comes to raising happy and healthy kids. Now I understand that it's not about how many people are in your team but what they've got to offer. But every time I read those negative messages a tiny dark cloud makes its way into my brain and I allow the comments to creep in. 'A single-parent family is dysfunctional, a single-parent family isn't a family, a single-parent family isn't ideal. My son would be better off in a two-parent family . . .' my brain tells me. That's very specific mum guilt and a very different kind to 'Oh but *are* Ella's Kitchen pouches really the same as freshly puréed?' The thought: 'Children of single parents are more likely to commit suicide' is a whole world away from: 'Will shoes that aren't from Clarks squeeze his toes?' And we just DON'T need it.

Think about it; I didn't exactly put in the order to be a single mum. I wasn't the one who opted out – that decision was very much out of my hands, not my area, control 100 per cent GONE. And in the same way, anyone could suddenly lose control of their so-called nuclear family and end up flying solo just like me. Worse still, anyone could lose a partner; widows and widowers make up a large percentage of single parents. I've learned quickly that high horses are SO not chic. Plus, of COURSE it's possible to find these trends, the 'empirical evidence' these angry types love shoving in my face – it's called socioeconomics, not evidence that single-parent families fundamentally can't work. However, shock horror, some people now are opting to be single parents. Some women are having IVF and planning their own single-parent families while some single men are using surrogates. How lucky you are when it comes to finding partners is no longer the deciding factor whether or not you can be a parent. As our methods of conception become more diverse, so too do our family set-ups. It's called PROGRESS. With the necessary support, being a single mother or father by choice can be not only manageable but a dream come true. Why should your relationship status get in the way of motherhood, if you are able to provide a stable and loving home? Love is the most important thing. All in all, the treatment, tests, drugs and sperm of IVF can cost £10,000. So rather than the reckless, poverty-stricken single mum of the *Daily Mail* stereotype, these are women who have serious cash in their pocket. For them, happy ever after doesn't involve a partner and is their very own normal. And it is just as likely to be successful as a traditional family set-up.

The typical theory endlessly presented to me by the single mum haters is that above all a child needs a mother AND a father, regardless of ANYTHING else. And therefore, having not provided this, I should feel eternally guilty, with a good old dollop of self-loathing thrown in for good measure. But the truth of the matter is that Freddy has got love firing at him from all angles. More than enough. I can't feel guilty for depriving him of love and support when he's rolling in the stuff. Yeah, he might not have a 'dad' but if we would just stop slapping labels on every damn thing then why would this even matter? He lives a life full and buzzing with people who love him and that's what counts way more than who he addresses his Father's Day card to.

Mum guilt is part and parcel of the birthing plan; it arrives as soon as the little blue lines appear on the pregnancy test. But if you know that you are doing the absolute best job you can at all times, then what's there to feel guilty about? The only time I feel guilty is when I let Freddy get in my bed and watch four episodes of *Bing Bunny* in a row so I can sleep in a bit longer in the morning. There was also the time he watched *Minions* twice in a row and ended up at nursery two hours, OK three, later than usual. He missed the 10.30 a.m. snack and I felt like the worst mother in the world. For a whole week after I set my alarm for 6 a.m. every day and cleaned the kitchen and put the slow cooker on before he'd even woken up just to rebalance. OK, two days . . . but it's the thought that counts.

But unintentional Netflix binges aside and despite the absent dad, the little *Minions* maniac is growing up to be a rather brilliant boy. Mother's bias that may be, but he's doing excep-tionally well at the old life thing so far. So why is it assumed that I am not proud of being his mum? The perception is that single mums shouldn't be proud; they should be ashamed for not convincing some bloke there was anything worth hanging around for.

I'm doing OK, y'know. I've got a job, I've written for the actual *Guardian* AND had my photo taken especially for it. I've bought a car – on finance but whatever – and have never been in police custody and I have never forgotten to dress him up for World Book Day. Even though one year we did technically forget but improvised with a wedding suit and a bow tie and he went as Doctor Who. And OK, I did bring shop-bought fondant fancies to the nursery Comic Relief bake sale, a fact of which I'm not proud. Even though they were from M&S and I did take them out the pack and cling film them myself. But I am proud of the little boy I've created – and out of all that degree, job, car-buying, article-writing nonsense, he is my proudest achievement. And I've interviewed Hanson. Sometimes, well actually every single night, I sneak in his room and watch him sleeping and can't believe what a perfect human I've made.

You see, I don't doubt myself because it's just me making the decisions. Having two humans as the face of the brand doesn't mean double the confidence. I don't doubt my capabilities as a mother just because I don't have a parental sidekick. Robson would have been just fine without Jerome. Look at all those fish he managed to catch on his own. I believe in myself as a mum as much as Cher believes in life after love. If anything, I doubt myself less because I have no one to question my decisions.

That's not to say having a child doesn't overwhelm the crap out of me sometimes, but I am no less clued up than any other first-time mum. Every time someone says, 'You are doing so well considering everything,' what it feels like it really means is, 'I didn't expect you to be doing so well.' It's well intentioned but the subtext is that because my life hasn't imploded, I am an exception to the rule. When really, anyone in any circumstance has the aptitude to be a kickass parent to their child. Doing this thing on my own doesn't remove my capacity to support and love my child unconditionally to the moon and back. 'I'm so proud of what you've managed to do,' friends will say, with the underlying assumption being that young, single mums don't achieve, they don't reach their goals, and when they do it's a surprise.

Even 'you look amazing' has to be followed up with 'especially for someone who has had a baby'. It's just one horrid rollercoaster of a sentence. One minute you are up and then whoosh – straight back down again. Erm, what exactly does someone 'who has had a baby' look like by definition? Vagina hanging out, permanent expression of pained regret framed by incurable dark circles round the eyes? Because once the cat is out the bag that you've pushed a life out from between your thighs, everyone seems awfully surprised when you look sort of all right. Mums scrub up OK sometimes too, y'know. Either that or we've just got our filters sorted.

Actually, that's one of the beauties of accidentally having a baby when I was twenty-four – I've got pretty much nothing to show for it. Except for the baby and a lot less money. But physically speaking, I'm not much different, really. Everyone I know who left it a little later seems to have something to complain about – whether it be stretch marks or a flabby tummy bit that just won't budge. God, I sound like a smug wanker right now. But most of those women have husbands so give me my small mercy, please. I'm lucky because I have actually pretty good muscle memory (hashtag blessed). I went to stage school until I was sixteen and we'd dance for about three hours every single day, which whipped us into excellent shape. As a result, I've always found it easy to get my body trim doing exercise. Saying that, I also didn't go for an eye test until Freddy was almost a year old so perhaps I just missed the worst of it.

And on the note of being twenty-four when I had my son – our society also has a huge issue when it comes to the age you become a parent. Despite most of my generation's parents being around my age when they had their first child, now it's expected that women should wait longer or suffer dire consequences. Although there is no wrong time to have children, and your children really don't know or care how old you are, the media seems hellbent on the idea that all women work through their twenties and thirties, freeze their eggs and settle down in their forties. Meanwhile, men are too busy being babies themselves to want to have them.

I was socialised to see my twenties as a time to explore myself, sleep with strangers, drink, travel, be irresponsible and selfish. Having children was seen as 'settling down', and it was drilled into me that I couldn't possibly be ready and actively seek this in my twenties unless I was a total dullard or hardcore Christian. The number of candles you had on your last birthday cake shapes the way society views you as a mother and not always for the good. There is an assumption that if you are on the younger end of mothers, that you must be 'troubled' in some way. So I expected to be miserable.

'First-time mum? But you look so young to have a baby!' was said to me almost daily when Freddy was little. This thinly veiled judgemental weigh-up was usually followed with: 'Was it a surprise?' Turn the tables for a second and imagine asking a stranger: 'Aren't you a bit old to be a mum?' Health visitors would say: 'You can tell me if it's a struggle,' offering me sympathy where it really wasn't needed, prodding away, convinced there must be some cause for concern that could eventually be prized out and presented to social services or a Radio 5 Live mental health phone-in. Most recently, I was mistaken for Freddy's au pair at his nursery summer party. Seeing a woman under thirty with a child made my fellow mum think I could only be the hired help. Not that I blame her. The only time we see a mother under thirty, they are portrayed as 'struggling' or 'troubled' in some way. They certainly aren't sharing your Laura Ashley picnic rug at the posh private nursery.

More recently, three-year-old Freddy was mid-meltdown on a flight to Spain. Screaming to leave his seat, repeatedly taking the seatbelt off and slamming the tray table up and down, if he were an adult they would have emergency landed the plane. He was at the full-on pissed-up stag do level of uncivilised. I tried every bargaining tool in my arsenal – snacks, sticker books, I even got out the iPad (lol who am I kidding – the iPad was out from the off) – but he was a young man on a mission. The performance's grand finale saw a Hot Wheels car take flight and hit a fellow child passenger in the face. The majority of our inflight audience looked on with a combination of dismay and disgust, at which point air rage momentarily took over, prompting me to ask, 'What do YOU suggest?' to one especially sour-faced old gentleman who had been particularly interested in my inability to control my struggling toddler.

If you are or look young, and you are on your own with a tantrumming child, the instant assumption is that you have lost control. Your parenting skills are questioned; it can't just be that you have a tired toddler. Parenting is tough, exhausting, mentally and physically draining however many years you have been on the planet and the last thing anyone needs is someone asking how old you are. However, I don't think anyone ever paid to look older so really, I'm winning.

Motherhood hasn't transformed who I am. Unfortunately – or perhaps fortunately – the mum bit is an add-on. I still get embarrassed, make mistakes, take knocks, drink too much, feel shy and self-conscious. Only now I am not just representing me, I am representing two people, meaning any judgement hits where it hurts the most. It's surely common sense that the mum who feels encouraged and praised in her parenting abilities will do a better job than one who feels judged by those around her? Whether there's one, two or twenty-two of you, this isn't what defines great parenting.

In an attempt to distance myself from this entire nasty stigma, now I try to think of myself more as a 'solo parent'. New Age, I know. Researching a piece I wrote for the *Guardian*, I stumbled (I say stumbled, I mean Googled) across articles about the prevalence of solo parenting in Denmark. These are self-elected single parents, where the children only have a relationship with one parent out of choice. Studies into these families have found no difference between the children of these women and children with two parents, in terms of psychological wellbeing. They found instead that the most important factor when it came to childhood adjustment was financial and social support. Well yeah, it seems like pure common sense when you put it like that. Denmark also has the highest employment rate of mothers in the world, state-funded nurseries and an amazing, supportive welfare system. Danish pastries are also the best things ever. Basically, what children don't need or respond well to is disruption, so if your child is healthy, happy and settled, then their parental set-up is kind of irrelevant.

My main fear is what living in a world that seems so set in its ways will do to my son's currently carefree, worry-less mindset. Don't children raised by two parents have twice the love, attention and resources than children raised by just one parent? That's what LBC radio presenter Andrew Castle said during one of his phone-ins on single parenthood, didn't he? It's the bad rep of single mums that makes me anxious. But then again, think how long it took for people to get into kale and online shopping. Come on, people, it's time to change for the better. Remember how shit life was before Amazon Prime? Exactly.

### Single Mum Myths Busted

1. **We're rich**

    **MYTH:** We suck money out of the government and are the reason your granny can't get a GP appointment and the NHS is crumbling.

    **TRUTH:** Look at the price of a family ticket to Legoland vs a single adult and a child and tell me who's winning.

## 2. We're poor

**MYTH:** Our kids look like Tiny Tim and are shivering in our unheated house as we reheat yesterday's baked beans.

**TRUTH:** Just like ANY group of people: some got the dollar, some don't. But I'm sure single mum Myleene Klass isn't scrimping.

## 3. We're lonely

**MYTH:** All we want is a bloke to complete our much-lacking family unit.

**TRUTH:** Our family is as complete as yours and we're not in a rush to add to it. PLOT TWIST, I know.

## 4. We want your husband

**MYTH:** Strapped for time and options, we are chirpsing up your husbands at the school gates.

**TRUTH:** The grass ain't greener when it features no hair and a middle-aged spread.

## 5. We're guilty

**MYTH:** I've failed my son and must feel eternal guilt for depriving him of a father figure.

**TRUTH:** Disruption is what causes problems, not the number of parents you have. Take your misleading stats elsewhere, please.

6. **We don't work**

   **MYTH:** We lounge around all day ordering gold bars off Amazon Prime, while our exes work only to give all their hard-earned cash to us.

   **TRUTH:** Single mums are as likely to be in work as their childless counterparts.

7. **We aren't proud**

   **MYTH:** We're ashamed of our poor decision-making skills that landed us in this 'mess'.

   **TRUTH:** I'm SO proud of the parent I never imagined in a zillion years that I'd become, if you stuck a pin in me I'd explode with pride.

# 7

# MUMMY, I SHRUNK YOUR TITS

oly guacamole: I was someone's mum. My name was 'Mum'. 'Hi, it's me, Mum – which life choice can I assist you with today?' Someone had found themselves stuck with ME to call their mama, to rep their brand until the age of eighteen. How had the wreckhead I formerly knew as myself become THIS? I suddenly really didn't recognise myself any more. Motherhood was panning out to be a real Britney shaved-head moment and I was having the ultimate identity crisis.

Identity by definition is the distinguishing character or personality of an individual (thanks, Google). And I was having an internal tug of war between 'Lindsay Lohan-esque twentysomething singleton' vs 'home counties Per Una-wearing mother of the year contender'. I didn't know whether I should be next to a bar or next to an Aga. Happy hour or happy meal? Ugh – even reading the word 'mum' made me instantly disenfranchise. I'd even catch myself saying things like 'Oh yeah, well that's for mums' about, say, a class at the gym – it having slipped my mind that I was now a mum and THIS was what mums look like.

Transitioning from carefree (ish) twentysomething to someone's actual mum was intended to be straightforward. Straightforward in the sense I would just deny it was happening for nine months and go to Lovebox festival. Out of sight, out of mind, and all that. An increasing bump did eventually come very much into sight, but even then, until my baby arrived I didn't properly 'get' what a shift was about to take place. First, let's get physical like Olivia Newton-John and talk the post-baby body transformation. Grab your legwarmers, people – and perhaps something to vomit into.

## Bean bag tits

To kick things off, let's talk tits. I've never particularly loved mine, but I've also never had reason to not like them. Basically, they were a long-time moot body part that I was neither here nor there with. Pregnancy and birth gave me lots of reasons to both like, love and then hate my tits. By heck, it fast became quite the rollercoaster relationship. When I got pregnant, I woke up with the tits of my dreams. It was like the *Zoo* model fairy had been to visit overnight. These stayed with me until I gave birth, although they were slightly undermined and over-shadowed by the whole baby-in-my-womb thing, meaning I never really got to make the most of them. Post-birth my tits became udders. Parts previously reserved to make dresses look decent and exercise uncomfortable were suddenly property of a little milk leech. I felt like I was on *Faking It* living the life of a cow.

## Got milk?

Next, let's talk about the milk coming in, shall we? Because no one does – probably because anyone who's been through it has attempted to repress the memories. Imagine how you feel when you REALLY need the loo – your bladder is so full that it's uncomfortable. Transfer that feeling to your tits. A big, full bladder each side slowly filling up until they can fill no more and unless you milk yourself, they will spurt out against your will. Meaning that you must wear tiny little sanitary towels over your nipples, just in case.

Three days into my new life as a cow, I started to feel hot. This heat fast turned into peaky until hot and peaky turned into flu-ey. Surely not? Surely I couldn't have got the bloody flu at a time like this? I'd only had it once before and it turned out that was glandular fever – so actually, I'd never had the flu before. So why NOW? Sodding sod's law, much? I fastened my tiny human into his car seat to make him portable and went to camp out in the Hemel Hempstead Urgent Care Centre. Feeling unwell when you are in charge of yourself is bad enough, but being on the frontline of two people's welfare doubled the pain. However, kudos to Hemel Hempstead Urgent Care as we were seen within about half an hour. I told the doctor my symptoms and that I thought I had the flu. They took one glance at the baby-filled car seat, another at my leaky boobs and told me I didn't have the flu. Turns out, I had mastitis. The curse of the very, very new mum.

Mastitis is basically infected milk ducts. My milk had gone mouldy because I had just so much. No baby could stomach all that lot so stuck it got. Girls with curdled milk don't cruise Tinder and go on holiday to Ibiza, do they? I felt very lost in my own body. Very lost and also very achy from flu, sorry, mastitis – flu of the mother. It felt like yet more punishment for that tiny bit of sex I had however many moons ago.

I breastfed for six weeks. I would have done longer but I just had SO much milk. I would be lying if I said I didn't look into selling it on eBay. But full-to-the-brim-with-milk tits are just agony and I couldn't take it any more so I abandoned the dreams of starting my one-woman human cream factory. After close investigation I concluded it was arguably more trouble than it was worth. I'd have to express – a.k.a. pump my own tits – in the middle of the night sometimes after they woke me up.

I chose to exclusively pump because, living at home, I quickly had quite enough of getting my boobs out in front of my parents. He's no Nigel Farage in Claridges telling me to get in the corner under a blanket, but I knew my dear old dad didn't know where to look when faced with his daughter's oversized nipples. He'd used up all his liberal points letting his unmarried knocked-up daughter move back home rent-free. Some things you might be able to do in front of total strangers but in front of your parents . . . not ideal. In this category are things like flirting and nightclub dancing. And, for me, breastfeeding. And before you have me down as the person who kicked that poor woman out of Claridge's, I would have been fine on the bus, in a café or in any other random-filled space – it was just mixing the visuals of my swollen breasts in front of my parents that I didn't take to so much.

So I took to tying a massive muslin cloth over me and using an electric breast pump under it so I'd always have milk at the ready. Yes, I could have probably hidden the baby under the muslin but no one wants to eat lunch in a balaclava, do they? A few times my parents would bring the neighbours in for a nightcap only to be greeted by the human milking station I had set up at the kitchen top. In fact, it soon became common-place and the dulcet sounds of the Medela Swing soon became standard background noise in our household.

But forever milking oneself? Ain't no one got time for that. I figured I'd done the hard graft – given the bambino all the good colostrum – so Auntie Aptamil could take over from here. Colostrum, by the way, is the real good stuff – the body's spun gold that comes out before your milk as soon as you've given birth. It's packed full of antibodies and other wondrous stuff to get your baby off to the best start and to protect him from nasties. But, for me, I had to stop after six weeks – my tits were oo big that even three sports bras couldn't hold them down. If they'd been permanent I would have angled for an NHS breast reduction.

Soon, though, I realised you need to be careful what you wish for. Someone somewhere had obviously been listening to my big boob cursing, my wishes for taxpayer-funded plastic surgery – because as the Lord giveth, so He doth taketh away. Mummy, I shrunk your tits. I shrunk your tits and left you with two half-empty beanbags. I also found my mood plummeted as soon as I stopped breastfeeding – the change in hormones sent me downward and for a while I would try and pump just one bottle a day and just throw it down the drain in an attempt to stall the hormonal dip.

Now my tits are my worst body part, really and truly. Kids, they steal your boobs – that's just a fact. Think, if you will, of a balloon that you inflate, inflate and inflate before letting go – of course the balloon isn't going to look quite the same at the end. And yeah, I know skin supposedly has loads of elasticity but I don't think my tits got the bulk of the collagen judging by the end result. I've tried push-up bras but the fullness just isn't there to push any more. I often daydream about booking flights and going to get a Bulgarian boob job but then I remember I don't have any money. Saying that, I did actually enjoy breastfeeding the rare times I was actually doing it. Seeing that little sucker attached to me and so peaceful really did bond us even tighter during those early days (and nights). If the living situation had been different I probably would have laid off the pump and gone au naturel.

## Not-so-designer vagina

Now, on to the big one. The one that had everyone worried. The one that would NEVER be the same again. Namely, my vagina. I'm going to keep this short and sweet for two reasons: 1) for the benefit of those of a sensitive disposition, and 2) for the diginity of my family name. Here goes: it's all right, but it's not exactly the same. There you have it. It works properly, but my gut feeling knows that it's not a carbon copy of pre-baby bits.

After giving birth and being stitched up, I wasn't keen on even looking down there. In fact, I just wanted to ignore that I even had genitals for the time being. Like fuck did I want to pee out of them. Unfortunately, boycotting peeing is a physical impossibility. So I had to grit my teeth and let it go. Think waterfalls, running streams, cute little brooks – NO, ALL I CAN THINK IS BEE STINGS, SUNBURN, RAW FLESH. Forget wiping anything, it was drip dry ALL the way. Apparently the John Legend's missus and model Chrissy Teigen reckons you can buy a little squirty bottle to clean up the area – like a post-birth portable bidet. Next time, I'll be equipping myself with one of those. Sorry, did I say next time? Excuse me, that was my temporary insanity talking.

## Stretch Armstrong

I was determined that 'my' physical identity did NOT include stretch marks – I was not going to see my identity change. But unfortunately for me, the act of creating a human plus nine months of KFC does change your body. Changes it to the tune of three stone, in fact. I'll lay it out flat and clear as day for you so you know what to expect. And just as you know that, if you are single, also know that you WILL pull again. Even though probably, right now, that is very much the last thing on your mind.

We are told to embrace change but I think whoever said that hasn't had a post-birth four-week-long period. I got PILES. Like, come on. I was twenty-four years old and fabulous ten months ago – WHAT THE FUCK WAS THIS? I didn't even know what piles were – so obviously initially I thought I was dying. I still can't get my head around the fact that something as teeny as a p in a v can create a shift of this magnitude. Like, people have sex all the time. If this is a possibility, you'd think no one would want to do it ever again. That it would go out of fashion as quickly as the trouser skirt.

## 99 Throblems

Next up from the alien body from hell agenda – everything throbs. I remember walking to Tesco from my house to fetch maternity pads, no less, and having to get a taxi back just to take the load off my healing, bleeding, Frankenstein vagina. This new version of me also had period pains for a frankly uncivilised amount of time after giving birth. Apparently, it was my womb shrinking back down to size. My gynaecological situation hadn't been given so much attention since the big period at the start of '02 when my mum shoved a sani pad in my hand and told me to hope for the best.

I daren't press my middle for about a week, knowing that the muscles had 'separated' during pregnancy – so gross – however, three years in, my middle is stronger and more defined than it ever was before albeit with the teeny tiniest bit of loose skin. Post-birth it was less toned, more coned. It used to literally raise up like Tower Bridge whenever I would attempt a sit-up.

During that time, I felt like I'd lost control of my body and I didn't recognise myself. I remember reaching for a formerly regularly worn long-sleeved bodycon dress, thinking that my womb had done all the shrinking it needed to do. As I pulled it over my head, the seams in the upper arms strained like they had never done before. Despite this, I persevered, and I managed to tug it down my torso until one side literally split at the seams. It turned out I still had a long way to go. I also had a wonky stripe down my middle, called a linea nigra – however, after a few months that was gone too. I still wonder if people with twins have two. None of my clothes fitted but I refused to buy anything other than my previous dress size – because I kept telling myself that this body was temporary. As a result, I lived in my maternity jeans for the first month after giving birth.

Being single during this post-birth time was, for me, definitely a blessing in disguise. I know most people say they get 'comfortable' and gain weight when they are in a relationship but historically I am at my most neurotic when I am with a guy. So for me, I felt like I could relax and heal totally in my own time during this period. I'm sure loads of coupled-up mums feel the same but I'm also fairly certain I would have been more inclined to speed up the getting-my-body-back process if my boyfriend was my audience instead of my dad.

That said, I'm never going to be one of these women who embraces the changes in their body, and says they are proud of what their bodies can do. Yeah, my body did an excellent human-making job but if I could maintain the body of my twenty-year-old self forever – well, who wouldn't do that too? Not that I'd keep the neurotic, insecure brain of my twenty-year-old self – she could stay put in yesteryear. But her tits – I'd have those. I wish I could be one of those people who say tummy rolls are 'beautiful reminders of the journey into motherhood' (ugh) but unfortunately I played with a LOT of Barbies growing up. Wellness experts can tell me until they're blue in the face that I am a 'superwoman' but all things considered I'd rather look in the mirror and see abs over cellulite. That might mean that my body image ain't all that but that's just the way I am, sadly.

I felt like a stranger in this bigger body and, after I'd given myself time to get over the birth, eventually I started to feel that it was making me unhappy. The only 'pressure' I felt was from myself. So I started to make changes. Hello gym with a crèche. This was a perfect way to spend maternity leave – I had time on my hands and no mum friends to hang out with then so the gym was the perfect antidote. Anyone who says you can't get your body looking pretty OK after having a baby hasn't worked out for two hours a day. I couldn't change my body back to exactly how it was before but I could change it into something I liked the look of. But really though, perfection is always pending – just like it was pre-baby.

The first time I went back to the gym for an aerobics class I promptly pissed myself. Post-baby incontinence is very real and at the gym, you'll know about it. I also had to forget trampolines for a while and even this year, THREE YEARS later, I still wear a just-in-case Tena Lady whenever I take Freddy to Bounce. It's a cruel irony to mothers that trampoline parks are just so popular at the moment.

But when I wasn't panicking about my gusset, the gym gave me time to think, evaluate and sweat – really, really, sweat.

When I'm in the gym, I feel suspended from the worries and blah of real life. It's a bit like when you're locked into a long-haul flight – for however long, it's just you and your workout. In this sense, it's absolutely as much about my mental health as physical. If you haven't got a gym membership – granted they do rinse your cash – then I would recommend Freeletics. It's an app you download and teaches you super-fast, super-effective HIIT workouts. My body inspo is a lady called lisamiller. fitness on Instagram – a single mum with a body that would have traffic hurtling off the road. She's fit, healthy and totally had a baby just like me. Meanwhile, Freddy had a whale of a time in the crèche and learned to be without me here and there which is probably one of the reasons he's never been a particularly clingy child and is a total three year old socialite.

All that sweat led to me getting back to the size I was before all this madness six months after giving birth. I felt so proud that I could make a baby and keep my body in shape. I think I exercised myself back to normality. I exercised my way back to having control over my body, the control I felt I had lost so much of.

Plus, those delicious exercise endorphins – let's just talk about them for a sec. I know that a workout can leave me in a good mood, however much I have to drag myself to it to start with. Exercise, for me, is the best antidepressant I've ever tried and, after becoming a mum, it became more important than ever.

Overall, somehow I ended up lighter and slimmer than before I had a baby. Even my face had a downsize – thanks, hormones, for those small mercies. But really what it all taught me is that everyone is different. Chrissy Teign got stretchmarks but I didn't even get one – but I did sacrifice my tits. However, I gained a thinner face so all's well that ends well.

But on the flip side, I'm also a massive, lazy cow. I think before I had Freddy, 'sleep' would have been a big definer of who I was. I still maintain I need eight and a half hours, preferably nine, to feel really ready to get up. I think if I were dying my final wish would be goose down pillows and nine uninterrupted hours. Sleep, and KFC, are legit my favourite things about being a human – so to have this whipped away from me and compromised was never going to be nice. I remember panicking about this a lot during pregnancy when I would try and cram as much sleep in as possible and make the most of the last of it. It was like sunbathing on the last day of your holiday and staying out until the very last second before you have to get on the plane. Sleep was my favourite thing EVER.

Now it was dictated by a miniature sleep Führer. I wasn't used to being tired like this. I genuinely did like night feeding, and still really cherish the memory of it feeling like we were the only two people awake in the world. But I still haven't quite adjusted to being on call 24/7 to an unpredictable human alarm clock. Plus, I had no second-in-command I could elbow when I really couldn't face being prised from the mattress. In some senses this was good because I knew for sure it was only ME that was being woken up so there was no stress or strain about who exactly had done what and who was pulling their weight. But that was only because I was pulling all the bloody weight.

Unbroken sleep just didn't happen for the first, well, year or two. I couldn't convince anyone to babysit overnight until Freddy was sleeping through the night. That happened shortly before his THIRD birthday. That meant a three-year sentence of human alarm clock minefield. You do just get used to feeling a bit shit all the time. A bit shit becomes your new normal. My advice to anyone who hasn't had a baby yet is to sleep like a drunk on the night tube and make the most of the precious deliciousness of the wondrous Zzzs: ride the Circle Line ALL night long before your sentence begins. Once your unbroken nights are few and far between you fantasise about the luxury of waking up naturally, or even to just a normal alarm clock. The idea of even having to set an alarm clock seems faintly orgasmic.

I started using and abusing coffee for the first time in my life. Forget what novelty Prosecco glasses tell us, COFFEE is mum juice, designed to convince us we are fully functioning members of society. Coffee can convince even the grumpiest of the grumpy – Grumpy Cat himself – that they are in a good mood. Well, for all of about twenty-seven minutes anyway. That's why there are so many of us camping out in coffee shops – because we are bloody knackered and just want twenty-seven minutes of human time. And that's why we meet other mums in coffee shops too – because otherwise we might simply fall asleep mid sentence.

It's not forever, so remembering that there's a light at the end of the tunnel should help you get through it. Even if, at the time, you feel like your eyeballs have dried up you are so knackered. My mother did make one exception to this no-over-night rule – when I was asked to report from the MTV European Music Awards in Glasgow when Freddy was about four months old. After the awards red carpet bit was over I didn't even go for a drink with my cameraman (sorry, Phil). While all the other journos were off trying to see which after-parties they could sneak into or what reality TV star they could snog, I just raced back to the hotel, whacked on the Do Not Disturb and fell into the most delicious sleep of perhaps my LIFE. My first uninterrupted sleep since the gigantic womb deflated – meaning I could sleep on my front, another one of life's most under-rated pleasures. That was probably one of the best holidays of my life. Well, apart from being fined by Glasgow police for putting a cigarette out in a pile of cigarette butts – however, that's an injustice for another time. Sorry, did I say holiday? I mean very hard day's work. Hard day's work interviewing The Hoff and sleeping in a lovely hotel room. I returned home more refreshed than any spa treatment could manage. Sleep really is the elixir of life, as anyone who's had it whipped away from them will testify.

Meanwhile, on the old mental front – in the brain box depart-ment – I was split. In the early days, I'd flip between being a total mum-slogan-jumper-wearing embracer of my new reality, to full-on denier who'd pretend to daydream about tequila shots because I felt like I had to (not that I ever really liked them anyway). I just didn't feel part of the mum tribe but I also no longer felt part of my old tribe. Basically, I didn't know where I fitted. I was a misfit new mother.

As had become a trend during pregnancy, I felt like I had to strive to cling on to the mast of the good ship Carefree and Single. I wanted to think that frumpy mum (soz, mums, I was dumb and ignorant) was just not me. I WOULD have my cake and eat it – just you watch. Yeah, that was never going to happen, was it? I think part of this was to do with my certainty that the mum cohort wouldn't accept me. Well, I was a fluffy idiot who had got pregnant very much by accident – 'Whoops! I'm having a baby!' – so what would I have in common with them? They wanted this; some had probably fought really hard for it and done five rounds of very expensive IVF. Whereas I'd just fallen into it. I didn't deserve association with proper mums, I thought. I was a banana skin slip of a mother so instead, I'd just pretend I wasn't one altogether. I was loving my role as a mum, I just wasn't sure what type I was yet. So in the meantime, I would outwardly deny all knowledge of it. Inwardly, I was a very happy mum, trust me.

There is a particular parenting website *ahem* Buzzfeed which seems to love nothing more than running numbered features with headlines such as, '22 things you won't do now you have kids', '8 things only twentysomething childless singletons can do' and '32 ways your life will never be the same after a baby'. Headlines which, after a while, feel akin to '22 ways having a baby is like being in prison'. I'll be having a great day when one of these articles, intended to be light-hearted yet DEEPLY OFFENSIVE, will pop up on my Facebook timeline and I suddenly feel like my day could be even better – if I didn't have a baby. THANKS A LOT. Headlines that make people who do have babies (a.k.a. me) feel the most intense FOMO even though I never massively liked clubbing or travelling particularly anyway. Well, I liked clubbing when I was drunk but then I'd probably like being in a bin when I was drunk.

Clubbing, drinking and travelling sum up all the things you can't do 'now you are a mum'. You're meant to spend your twenties doing THAT, not being knee-deep in muslin squares. Those articles make me feel like I'm not a 'proper' young person if I haven't done everything on that list. And I've done hardly ANY of the things on that list. Plus, even the things I have done, I haven't particularly enjoyed. And yeah, you probably don't believe me on the travelling front but it's true – I think it's because I'm scared of flying, hate airports and never remember my glasses when I go sightseeing – that's enough to put you off, trust me. Wanderlust is not a thing for me. Although sometimes I am tempted to put it on my Tinder profile because it sounds cool.

The first New Year's Eve after Freddy's birth was a decent summary of the dichotomy I faced. While, as you know, I was in love with my new role, I felt I should be drinking and clubbing and being all mid-twenties and 'fun'. I felt I owed it to my generation to WANT to be doing what all my friends were doing. To clarify, at this time absolutely zero of my friends had children.

NO ONE babysits on New Year's Eve so it's probably the one time the childful just have to accept they won't be going out. So the last few hours of 2014 were spent at home with my three-month-old baby son . . . who fell asleep at 8 p.m. The remainder of the night was spent with my mother debating whether Jools Holland wears a toupee. No one had to pretend to remember the words to 'Auld Lang Syne', and at midnight I knew exactly who I was going to kiss and it wasn't a random whose number I forgot to save. Honestly, I loved that New Year's Eve. It was calm and perfect, and I felt like I was exactly where I was supposed to be. Plus, the next day four of my friends came and visited us in Berkhamsted and we had a New Year's

Day lunch instead. I didn't miss out on anything, apart from the hangovers.

My New Year's resolution that year was to focus on the present, not the past and certainly not Facebook. While it's easy to say what life (or shots) you COULD be having, it's better to focus on the life you ARE having because that's the only one you've got. Well, duh really. Still, I swear I saw that on an inspirational canvas once. But still I felt the tug of my inner twenties demon shouting how I should have my feet stuck to the floor of an overpriced nightclub with someone shouting at me, 'COME ON, HAVE A DANCE!' That's how people – especially single people – have FUN and I wouldn't be any fun if I missed out, was the way I was thinking.

That all came to a sorry head the first night I was set loose back into the nighttime economy when Freddy was about four months old. Well, firstly I should explain that I hadn't drunk any alcohol for a VERY long time and even before my booze sabbatical I had been an appalling drinker. 'A sniff of the barmaid's apron' is enough to get me going, my friend Olly says. The second problem was that I didn't know what to wear. Nothing fit me properly any more and nothing felt like it ticked the 'mum undergoing identity crisis' box so I left feeling like I wish I'd picked something else. I also felt like everyone would judge me knowing that I was out on the sauce and my son was at home with my mum. However, I decided to combat this feeling with loads of drink. Social anxiety always gets better when doused with tequila, right?

So I drank like it was going out of fashion. Eventually I lost my friend and found myself surrounded by blurred faces, in the middle of my most entertaining story – the birth story, again – gesticulating like an over-excited conductor for extra emphasis, so much so that I gesticulated my glass flying. As it shattered on the floor I yelled something about flailing maxi sani pads. The blurred faces definitely didn't find this as hilarious as I did. I got to the part where Chris Tarrant has just got his fist ready – the blurred faces now looking very confused – and that, my friends, is where I blacked out.

The next thing I knew I had my hands in the crib and my mum was grabbing my waist from behind.

'Get off him RIGHT now, you STINK,' she said.

I was upstairs in my house, somehow having got home, but my shoes were still on and I had trailed mud up the stairs on the cream carpet. There was mud over the knees of my trousers too. I had no idea where my handbag was and I had recollections of walking all the way home from town. Hence the mud. OK, I was REALLY drunk. 'Khjkjhkijsdksakfj,' I mumbled back, still trying to get into the crib. Fred was none the wiser, dead to the world with his hands up in the little Mexican wave way he used to sleep then.

'You are an ACTUAL IDIOT. Now GET OUT.'

My mum prised me off the cot and as she pulled my hands my legs gave way and I face-planted into the rug beneath it. I only woke up when the poor offspring of a drunk started crying to be fed a couple of hours later. Every cry felt like splinters to the frontal cortex. CRYING SO LOUD. CRYING WITH NO MERCY.

Must. Find. Water. Desperate, I scanned the room. It was either micellar water or this. It would be better than the stairs. And so I swigged some of the Cow and Gate follow-on milk left out for Freddy's night feed. It was surprisingly delicious, a real silver lining to that regrettable cloud. With the sustenance of infant formula for fuel, I manage to lever myself onto the feeding chair, rocking my baby while seriously assessing my life choices. He stopped crying. Peace was restored.

I have only properly remembered the crib incident just now, the images coming back to me, flooding my cheeks red with shame.

The next day was distinctly awful, to make an understatement. My mother wouldn't talk to me, let alone help me, and caring for a baby after pumping yourself full of Woo Woo, well ... What? It was on offer, OK? Hangovers and childcare mix like oil and water. Added to the specific shame was the general anxiety that comes with hangovers of this proportion – hanxiety. My soul needed ironing. Who knows what could have happened if my mum hadn't woken up? I wasn't responsible, I wasn't a mother – I WAS an idiot, like my mum had said. Because this baby lark – it didn't magic me more responsible. I felt like I should be tarred and feathered and paraded through town. For all I remember, perhaps I had been. However, I'm only human, a lightweight human at that, so incidences with similar shades of this did occur again. But the shame never got any better; it never got any more internally acceptable to be a mum who can't handle her liquor. Freddy deserved better than a mother with inexplicable muddy clothes and a lost handbag.

When faced with hungover childcare, I liked to play: 'You be the mummy and I'll be the baby,' which involved a lot of lying down on my part. I also would play: 'You be the waiter and fetch Mummy some crisps,' or 'Mummy is poorly, you be the doctor and make her better' – which also involved a lot of horizontal time for Mummy. Freddy never complained, which made the guilt easier to stomach.

Would a husband have released me from the shackles of hungover parenting? Perhaps. But then he also probably wouldn't have been too buzzed about having a wife who once woke up with a bump on her forehead after telling her friends this was a 'naked taxi' and having to be restrained and head-butting a door frame while stripping off. And the only thing worse than a wife like that would be a mother like that.

Maybe I could just about get away with shit like that when I was just another single girl, but now I was a mum it all felt very different the next day. According to popular InstaMum chatter, the mum hangover is just one entry on the long check-list of 'shit mums have to do', but I just can't do it any more. I was a bad drunk and I'm an even worse mum drunk, so it felt like it was time to knock it on the head – I'm sure CBee-bies will stay in business without us propping up the viewing figures. When you do stupid shit drunk and you are a mother, everything multiplies – including the hungover regret. I felt like I was under one big magnifying glass of shame. For me, it wasn't worth it any more so now I only get REALLY drunk when I'm on holiday or at a festival – so basically, once a year when I'm VERY far away from my baby. Never the two shall mix again.

Of course the flip side of this stereotype of the loose cannon, livewire twentysomething wreckhead who just so happened to also be a mum was the other extreme: the female equivalent of

Peter Andre, all perfect parenting and 'I love my kid, everyone!' Cue plastered-on grin. Well, I really, really did, to be fair. So as soon as I took Freddy home from the hospital, I made a vow to myself to go totally Stanislavski on the role I'd just landed – the role of 'the mum'. I would live and breathe what life had taught me 'a mum' was. Mums were sensible, Mums were responsible. Mums were probably good at baking scones. Reading that back, no wonder I'd get so loopy drunk every so often. Mums wore comfortable but chic activewear and cooked things other than microwave meals. I signed up for every class – sensory, Music Bugs, baby yoga – we'd go a few times and then I'd panic that no one liked me and boycott it for the rest of the term. Freddy inevitably missed out but I just didn't know what to say or how to act with all the pressure I'd put on myself.

I met a mum at my gym crèche once and was so excited when she invited me to a local mum and baby group. It felt like the first day of school and I was determined to fit in. So I dressed the part. I wore black leggings and a plain top and toyed with the idea of Ugg boots before I realised maybe I was underselling the 'mum' archetype somewhat. It took me a long time to realise things might be easier if I was just MYSELF. Identity depends on your own view of yourself and my vision was skewed.

Since then, I've realised girls don't morph like chameleons into 'mums' and if you actually LOOK AROUND you will see there are pierced mums, tattooed mums, prim mums, trim mums – every kind of mum, because we are INDIVIDUALS. Duh, why did it take me so long to realise this? Loud mums, quiet mums, working mums, stay-at-home mums – goddammit, we've got our fingers in all the pies and every base is covered if you look hard enough. I thought once I became a mum and stepped over the line from the 'antenatal' to 'postnatal' that it would be the magic cure for self-consciousness. I had assumed that I would undergo a drastic confidence makeover because, well, mums weren't shy, were they? I thought of my mum when I was growing up – she wasn't ever shy of asking, shy of speaking up – heck, once she even got on stage with the *Sesame Street* gang after they picked her out the audience at a show. It's only after becoming a mum I realised you don't change, you just get better at acting, better at fronting. My own mum has since confessed she was terrified of being on stage with Big Bird – however, she admits 'he sounded really handsome from inside the suit' and had an American accent.

Being a mum is a lot of acting, especially when you are the sole face of the brand. Being confident in front of the nursery staff – all an act. Being confident in front of health visitors – all an act. Enjoying soft play – very much all an act. But you get good at this acting, you want to do it to give your little one the best chances possible. You can say 'do as I say not as I do' as much as you want, but ultimately you are your child's role model. So that's what pushed me into getting my act together, realising I was just as much of a mum as anyone else who had given birth and not all mums bake scones.

A new chapter meant a new chance to find what type of mum I REALLY was. Beanbag tits and all. And I even started to like the person I was – the mum I had become.

# 8

# MAMA'S GOT BILLS TO PAY

I was well into the nitty-gritty of a particularly uncomfortable routine smear test recently when the nurse asked, 'What do you do for work then?'

I hate being asked that question. I like it even less when I've got a miniature chimney sweep doing the rounds up my giblets. If I had it my way, there would be a little electric screen between us and I'd be very much putting it UP. Alas, somewhere between my interrogator lubing up the speculum and shoving the brush up I found myself here, being grilled by Nurse LinkedIn. Surely, there must be something in patient confidentiality about this? Alas, being British, I didn't want to offend so, 'I'm a journalist,' I said.

'Journalist? Oh God, I couldn't imagine anything worse than WRITING all day,' she replied. Still talking, still with her head between my legs.

I pretended to laugh and said something like, 'Oh right, yeah, well . . .' trailing off and willing for silence before I could be released to shuffle off for the next three years. But what I should have said was what I am going to tell you now . . .

From when I was a little girl, as long as I can remember, I wanted to be some kind of journalist. Whether it was writing stories or broadcasting them on the TV or the radio, I wanted to do it. Preferably involving celebrities because as an impressionable little girl in Hertfordshire, I rather loved those too. Their world just seemed so glamorous and covetable and – growing up on the outskirts of the neither glamorous nor covetable M25 – I wanted to be a part of it. I could say I had a thirst for breaking the stories that matter, but really I just wanted to mingle with famous people and break the stories that don't really matter but we love reading them the most. I am also very nosy and like finding out gossip I probably shouldn't know so I think this also contributed to my chosen profession, which has been a career of asking inappropriate questions.

I used to write my very own *Amy's News* newspaper, copying the layout from my nan's copy of the *News of the World*. When I wasn't reading up on things that I definitely shouldn't have been, despite the insistence it was a 'family newspaper', I was nicking my dad's Sony Handycam to film myself interviewing my Beanie Babies. I graduated from this to hosting my own radio show, recording it through the microphone on my family PC and putting it on floppy disks. When I was about thirteen my friend and I were in Leicester Square while the premiere for a Keira Knightley film called *King Arthur* was taking place and, pressed against the security barrier, opposite the press pen, I realised THAT was what I wanted to be – a person holding a microphone in front of a camera.

People other than the smear test nurse tend to ask quite a lot how I managed to actually get started in proper journalism. They might just be being polite and not actually care – but it's thanks to them I will fill you in. When I was a teenager I would have killed for this kind of intel so hopefully it will benefit someone somewhere who wants to grow up to play Buckaroo with a disgruntled Charlize Theron. Or, as my dad says, 'spend all day writing about Gok Wan's underpants'.

Back when I was in sixth form, my mum went to a New Year's Eve party and met Alessandra Steinherr who worked on the editorial team at *Glamour* magazine. She was there with her husband and they were shoved on a table with my mum and dad for the meal. My mum says they talked about politics a lot and made her feel very out of her depth when she didn't know who the French prime minister was. This was the closest that I or any of my family had ever got to the profession I wanted to break into so badly, so for us, it was like meeting the Queen. And the Queen told my mum that the key to this biz was getting work experience. I still can't believe my mother didn't then ask her if I could have some at *Glamour*. Alas, she says she 'didn't want to seem desperate'.

Inspired by this meeting, I decided this was what I needed to do – drop everything and get work experience immediately. But how many chumps must be asking for that? I thought. So with this in mind, I sent a shoe to about ten different editorial assistants (the Queen said this is who was best to contact first) with the message: 'Now I'm half way to getting my foot through the door.' Well, in truth, I sent an A4 print of a clip-art shoe – well, can you imagine how much the P&P would cost to send an actual shoe? Where do you even get single shoes? However, I do still lie about how I 'really thought outside the box and sent an actual shoe' to London's editorial teams – lauding it as perhaps my greatest creative moment. Phoning round various Pets at Home and asking if they had a cage that would fit a human in a video parody about Alex Reid's sex dungeon came a close second. That one actually did happen.

While I heard nothing from the majority, one editorial assistant took pity on my poor clip-art efforts and I was offered one week at *More!* magazine owned by Bauer Publishing – the home of my beloved *heat* magazine. I didn't read *More!* enough to know it for anything other than its infamous 'Position of the Week' where they would recreate sex positions with Barbies and manifest it as some sort of sexual instruction manual. I actually had to tidy up those Barbies at one point during the week and felt oddly starstuck. Being on my first-ever work experience placement, and in fact in my first-ever office, I was beyond nervous. So nervous, in fact, that I visibly shook trying to do the filing as if I were auditioning for *X Factor* and this was my one chance to impress.

The magazine was in a building of about ten different offices, each home to a different title – *heat* included – so knowing I probably wouldn't have such good access again anytime soon I hatched a plan to weasel my way into them all. Like a total brown nose who would now irritate me greatly, every time I got in the lift I would strike up conversation with whoever was in there, trying to bag a week or two at their title. Boyd Hilton at *heat* was one of my victims. See also Sam Delaney – the then editor of *heat* magazine – who probably, actually definitely, won't remember who I am. Sam Delaney introduced me to my absolute journo hero – Lucie Cave – who was known for everything I loved. She used to work on Trouble TV and had since become known as the person to be cheeky and funny but never mean when interviewing celebs. When I grew up, I wanted to be just like Lucie Cave. Yep, the lines between tenacious and fucking irritating were blurry during this time.

But my persistence paid off and I worked my way around that building at about five different magazines over the next four years, including after I'd gone off to university – the only one that wouldn't have me was *Grazia*, not that I blame them. I went to *FHM*, *Zoo*, *Q*, *Closer* and of course, *More!*, where I started. Don't tell Leeds University but sometimes I would bunk off whole weeks to go and make tea and coffee – and once make half-peanut butter half-Marmite toast – for London's editorial staff. If you worked on a magazine between 2008 and 2012 I probably made you tea and panicked over whether to take the tea bag out or not. I whored myself around Bauer Tower like I was ticking off a work experience bucket list. And yes, I even made it to my beloved *Heat*. They liked my desperation enough to let me start writing stories for the website from home while I was still at university.

Also on the web team with me was a girl called Giovanna. You'd know she was on shift because a McFly story would always pop up. Turns out it was only blimmin' Giovanna Falcone – now Fletcher – who went on to marry Tom from the band and become a mummy blogger extraordinaire. Whenever I have met her since, I have reminded her of our humble web writer beginnings at *heat*.

The majority of working journalists were expected to work for free at the start just like I did. For me, it was easy because I could stay at my parents and commute in every morning. I was still basically paying to work but only the daily train ticket. I've since wondered what would have happened if they'd lived further away. I could afford to be unpaid for a few weeks but certainly couldn't have paid for accommodation on top of that. Surely a job should be awarded for talent, not whether your parents have bankrolled you through unpaid work placements? Just a thought, anyway.

I also worked in the university call centre to fund all this back and forth – cold-calling former students to try to convince them that giving even more money to the university in the form of an alumni donation was a good idea. The lady I rung during the two-minute silence on Remembrance Day did not think it was a good idea. Explicitly so, in fact.

When I was not commuting between Leeds and London, I also made the most of the university media societies. I was the features editor of the uni paper where we'd run features like 'Reem and Scream Halloween Outfits' and 'Turn Your Walk of Shame into a Walk of Fame'. One week we put together a feature entitled 'Can You Dress Like a Celeb?' which involved sending one of our writers to Oceana in a dress made from raw bacon just like Lady Gaga's meat dress. Turns out only celebs can dress like celebs. People were just TAKING THE BACON. Quite literally. People covertly removed rashers of bacon from the dress and took them home with them. So yeah, that, added to the high risk of salmonella, left us concluding we should stick to Topshop like the Muggles we are.

I also teamed up with a very clever boy who has since pro-
duced for ITV, Channel 4 and loads of other dead good outlets
who worked out we could broadcast video on the student TV
and the audio on the radio. We – well, mainly he – saw how
live music would be perfect for this. So we started writing to
touring bands asking if we could come and film their shows
and then I would interview them afterwards. I was a rubbish
interviewer and would basically Google the band on the way to
the venue, which led to some truly cringe factual inaccuracies
like when I asked a folk singer if she would agree her genre
was 'classic rock and roll'. Despite me being acutely rubbish,
we actually filmed loads of relatively famous bands – Charlie
Simpson's Fightstar, The Holloways and one time we managed
to book Just Jack – that bloke who did that 'Stars in their Eyes'
song. We also interviewed a guy who had a tiny guitar with a
paw sticker on it and when he sung his cheeks went very red.
That man went on to become Ed Sheeran. OK, now I sound
like Forrest Gump. But it's true and still on YouTube. Well, I
say 'went on' but he was already Ed Sheeran. Just no one gave
a shit like they do now.

So before this starts to sound like a part-CV/part-*This Is Your
Life* montage slash namedropping marathon, I'll conclude by
saying that just before graduation I was offered a job at Yahoo
Celebrity – then called omg! – as a celebrity reporter. BUZZ. I
didn't know Yahoo was really a thing other than for old men to
check their emails but the words 'celebrity reporter' had me all
in a tizz. Plus, the fact they wanted to give me actual money
instead of working for free.

That first week I couldn't believe anyone could do this much cool stuff. I was being *paid* to write about and meet celebrities. On my second week my boss, Julia, asked me to report from the *Batman: The Dark Knight Rises* premiere and to ask everyone there who they would most like to see in a PVC catsuit. For the record, not my idea. I remember being surprised that the premiere organisers handed out a sheet with a picture of everyone who was invited and a little reminder of their name, to avoid any interview faux pas. But after a ten-year subscription to *Heat* magazine, I didn't need such a prompt. That day I asked the likes of Mark Wright, the late Peaches Geldof and the one that lives on a farm off JLS who they would most like to see in PVC. Life had peaked.

This was that start of asking celebrities weird things and for the next two years I would ask anyone just about anything unless their press representative interrupted first – which happened more often than you would expect. Unlike when you are asked a question in real life, celebrities have an automatic opt-out function – which normally manifests as a raised eyebrow to an otherwise silent accomplice who sits in as you interview. They even sit in on phone interviews and lurk there like a silent member of a WhatsApp group. Things I wasn't allowed to ask include: 'What does your ex smell like?' to Kelly Brook. 'Can you kiss this puppet?' to Cameron Diaz. 'Which member of One Direction would you most like to catch chlamydia off?' to Jedward. I was also banned by Sony from asking One Direction who, out of the five, is the best kisser. I was never given a reason for the blanket banning of any of these questions but I maintain the One Direction best kisser one is absolutely fair enough and I'm fairly certain I know what the answer is. Harry, duh. As I am a proper journalist, I would have been willing to put myself forward to find out.

Things I got away with asking, however: Robert Downey Junior if he wanted to come to Nando's. He didn't. Bradley Cooper to marry me. He didn't. Jennifer Aniston if she liked Doritos. She didn't. Ariana Grande which member of The Wanted she would go out with if Nathan Sykes (her then boy-friend) went missing indefinitely. Jay. I'd seen far too much *Balls of Steel* and basically thought I was Olivia Lee. One time I was interviewing Jedward when actual Jon Snow off Channel 4 news – not to be confused with Jon Snow off *Game of Thrones* – busted through the door telling us to SHUT UP. In a pure coincidence he was filming something in the same hotel.

I continued all this even as a heavily pregnant woman and would hide my expanding uterus behind the press pen barrier and go ahead and ask the questions that (didn't) matter. Just two weeks before I gave birth I asked Cilla Black old *Blind Date* questions and did impressions of Graham. After a particularly pregnant interview, Peter Andre took me to lunch and told me everything was going to be great. James Corden wished me luck, Tom and Dougie from McFly wrote Freddy a message for his arrival in the world in a copy of their children's book. Thinking about it, celebrities were actually the most supportive group of people during my pregnancy. Thank you to all of them. So once the baby was here, I was hardly just going to abandon this truly awesome ship. However, little did I know, I was about to get shoved off the ship anyway.

A few days before I was due to give birth it was the *TV Choice*

Awards and, not wanting to risk a birth in the press pen, I had agreed that a freelance presenter could take my place. All I could do was watch from home and scrutinise his performance, say he was rubbish to anyone who would listen while inwardly feeling convinced he was better than me. Reluctant to have to experience or risk this again, I vowed I wouldn't have anyone cover for me in future. And this is how I ended up back on the red carpet at the Pride of Britain Awards ten days after giving birth. I even had a really good idea for it. The tagline for the awards is 'Ordinary People Doing Extraordinary Things' so I decided to find out whether 'Extraordinary People' – i.e. the celebrities – could do ordinary things. I maintain, a seminal idea.

Arriving at the Royal Albert Hall, I had to take five in the women's loos to manually pump my own breasts for some relief. My boobs were like rock-hard swollen udders that no breast pads could contain. Stopping the celebs on their way down the red carpet, I asked them for directions to the nearest tube, I suggested they check their emails, I took satsumas to see if they could peel them. But the real pièce de résistance, if you ask me, was asking Simon Cowell to pull off a single sheet of toilet roll. I think it's still on YouTube somewhere. I remember one of the boys from Union J laughing and saying, 'It's never normal when you are around!' and I felt officially back in the game.

In the following months, I covered MOBOs, the BAFTAs and the Radio 1 Teen Awards and thought everything was back on track. I also went to the EMAs in Glasgow where I did all that sleeping. It was perfect; I was technically on maternity leave but then would work just at events – around two a month – during which time my mum would babysit for me. My toe was firmly still in the pool while I still had all the time to adjust to my new life at home. I was so proud that I was juggling, no, *bossing* my job and motherhood. I trust my Mum one million per cent – in fact, I mostly think Freddy is safer with her than he is with me, so I knew he was fine with her. That's the biggest worry when you go back to work – that your kid is in safe hands. Luckily, I knew for certain that he was, meaning I could totally switch on to the task in hand. That's not to say I didn't miss him oh so much – and still the best bit of any of those days was coming home to smell his little baby head afterwards. The loose plan was I would then go back to my full-time reporting job after my maternity leave was over.

However, then my boss Julia announced she was leaving to go and work at Twitter and the people left behind weren't all fans of the arrangement we'd had. The new bosses essentially cut all my red-carpet content and Julia's replacement started doing the remainder of all the other interviews herself. Fair play to her, I would have probably done the same. There are few people like my original boss Julia – she let me take chances and try out ideas even though they didn't always work and were sometimes terrible. But ultimately, she believed in me and never let her own ego get in the way. I was lucky to work with her as long as I did. Unlike SO many bosses, Julia really saw the strengths in her team and in herself and made the most of them. She also single-handedly made sure that I got the proper maternity pay I was entitled to – something that bought me precious time to work out what to do next. I would have had to rely on state maternity allowance if it hadn't been for her.

But now I'd lost my dream job and knew how few and far between opportunities like that were – especially when you can't work all hours of the day. I applied and interviewed for some full-time reporter positions on magazines and newspapers, which probably would have entailed some video work for their websites. But on working out the commute times and the nursery prices I realised it just wouldn't be feasible unless I was on about a hundred grand a year and that wasn't happening any time soon. To have a full-time job in London would mean dropping one-year-old Freddy off at nursery or a childminder at 7.30 a.m. and not picking him up again until 7.30 p.m. – that's twelve hours – just for a nine-to-five job. I couldn't yet afford to move – I could only just afford full-time nursery care. And in a job like I had, so much of what you do is out of hours: evening events, launches, parties. Stuff that does not compute with a young child.

It was an odd feeling to think that I couldn't just do whatever I wanted any more. My emphasis had always been on forging the career I wanted by being as flexible as possible and now I was very restricted. And in something as competitive as journalism, you can't be restricted. You are expected to work late, be available and quite often take on shifts, which include weekends. However, as my old nan always told me – as one door closes, a window opens.

I remembered what I had vowed to myself when I decided to have my baby – a baby doesn't change what you can do, it just changes when you can do it. My skills remained the same; I just had to work them around my new timetable. I stuck to thinking that if I were good enough, if I stood out enough from my competition, then I would find the right work for me. So what did I need? A job I could work around my baby. Which I soon found out is easier said than done. I realised I'd have to go freelance. I would TRANSFER my skills, as they say in recruitment.

But even this presented a problem, as I still needed to have the space and time to concentrate while working at home. Friends (without kids) would say: 'Why can't you just write while Freddy sleeps or plays?' The answer being, as anyone WITH kids will know, because he never sleeps or plays at the right damn time. So I had to outsource the childcare. I found a local child-minder called Shelley. Shelley's house became Freddy's second home easily and quickly. I just wish I could have come round to Shelley's house that day after I took all that MDMA. It was the epitome of cosy. With a family of five of her own, Shelley was used to dealing with chaos – but it was wholesome chaos. Shelley was the type of lady you know made the best packed lunch and didn't mind if you got a little bit of mud on the carpet. Their house was one of those houses you know is a proper home. I missed him but he was so happy; I was the only one suffering and I knew he was in the safest of hands.

With this arrangement in place, I called upon every contact I had made in journalism to investigate what 'freelance' was all about. Basically, it meant I had to convince editors to take my ideas. So this is what I set about doing with the same push as when I sent that clip-art shoe round to all those magazine offices previously. I managed slowly to build relationships with a handful of editors until I felt I could trust them to give me regular work, although it was never guaranteed. Having no guarantee of work was and still is a constant worry and there have admittedly been times my family have bailed me out of my cash-flow problems.

That's the problem with being a freelance anything – you have no guarantee of work. Which is probably why no one likes giving mortgages to self-employed people. Ask any freelancer and they'll tell you 50 per cent of the job is chasing invoices. If I got paid a quid for every time I had to send a friendly but firm email chasing an invoice I'd definitely have a deposit for a house saved up by now.

I also sent my showreel of my best inappropriate questions off to agents and eventually signed with one who puts me up not just for presenting jobs but also acting and 'commercial modelling jobs'. Basically, shoving my face in adverts. These are few and far between but if you actually get one then that's worth over half a year's pay in journalism. The girl on those Tesco delivery lorries looks a bit like me because, SURPRISE, that is me. Eating a beetroot salad with the tagline 'Freshly clicked' that my oh-so-supportive friends say is screaming out to be graffitied to 'Freshly dicked'. Getting these jobs involves going to 'castings' where you have to do things like 'smile with your eyes' and show your hands to the camera. I have probably been to about thirty castings and got about three jobs – though to be fair to myself, they are attended by sometimes HUNDREDS of people. At one casting to be in a Costa coffee advert a woman turned up in an actual Costa coffee uniform. Based on that alone, I would have given her the part.

The cash flow was still a bit of a problem though. The whole childcare costing more than rent – hence why I couldn't afford both – situation meant I couldn't depend on risking it with free-lance pitches that might not get picked up, so I needed to rack my brains for means of making cash that didn't involve two-hour commutes and nine-to-five contracts. To get a guaranteed regular income, I also started working part-time as a children's entertainer. I took my fancy dress from the red carpet and used it to shout party games through a megaphone at kids' birthday parties. I called myself Astro Amy and still, on occasion, dress up and teach kids how to launch lemonade rockets and make slime. It's great fun. It actually proved quite a lucrative racket and I've ended up taking it to festivals and shopping centres too. This single mum has a hella different strings to her bow. Well, you gotta hustle when childcare is 100 per cent geared up to be covered by two incomes and the UK allegedly has the most expensive childcare in the world.

My CV makes absolutely zero sense any more but I finally managed it so that I was making the same money as I would working regularly in an office, while also making it compatible with being a mum. I didn't realise when I decided to divide my time the way I have done, but I am essentially flexi-working. Being a working mum has taught me the importance of vari-able working hours. That is, working as hard as everyone else, just in the hours available and from home when I can. If an employer had been flexible, I probably would have taken a staff job – but the way things are, it wasn't an option. In this sense, I do feel slightly penalised by the workforce for having a baby.

I know that any mother is capable of achieving the career and education she wants but, for now, we are still fighting against the odds. Let's face it – a full-time job doesn't fit with the school run. Childcare can fall through or not work out as expected. Most of us would rather see our children for more than just an hour before bed each night. According to the charity Pregnant Then Screwed, 54,000 women every year are forced to leave their jobs early as a result of being sacked or made redundant after having a baby. I was advised by people I knew in senior roles not to mention I was a mum when interviewing for staff jobs as it could 'put people off'. And it's true, I wouldn't be able to stay late or work weekends easily. But that doesn't mean I have no value to an employer. The workforce isn't kind to mothers for daring to procreate and is suffering and losing talent as a result.

We're told women are leaving having children later due to choice but I think it's an illusion of choice. One of the main things I heard when I was pregnant was people saying they 'wanted to have a career first'. I think if I hadn't fallen pregnant when I did I would have been terrified to 'plan' a pregnancy at any point, in the belief my career would be snatched away. Indeed, when I was pregnant I was convinced my time was up and I'd have to revert to being a stay-at-home mum, most likely on benefits. This hardwired belief leaves women feeling insecure. They are 'holding on' for fear of losing the careers they've worked so hard for.

I didn't lose my career but I did have to adapt it and mould it round my new life as a mum. I was flexible where most jobs aren't but if more jobs were flexible then this would surely be just, well, better for everyone involved. While my priority will never be my job again, that doesn't mean I'm any less dedicated to it; I'm only ever getting better at it and gaining more experience with every passing year. A lot of books are written by people who have 'made it' – but not a lot of space is given to anyone who nearly did. I feel like I'm still nearly there; in fact I've hardly started and the best is yet to come. And now of course I'm sharing everything with my favourite miniature sidekick, and I want to make him proud more than I've ever wanted to make anyone proud, myself included. So I'm not giving up just yet, although realistically I think my CBBC dreams are on the scrapheap. Unless they open up a middle-age diversity campaign and then maybe I can shove my hat back in the ring. But it was becoming a parent that has made me happier than anything I've ever done or perhaps could do professionally . . . which leads me to a story about a celebrity you all MUST know unless you live in a (very boring) cave.

I was ten weeks pregnant when I was sent to interview Mel C. 'Please don't vomit on Sporty Spice,' I begged myself, battling morning sickness. I wasn't showing, but I was certainly feeling sick almost constantly, that is. But there was NO way I was going to bail on meeting my childhood hero. OK, fourth childhood hero. Because obviously in order of heroes it goes Geri, Baby, Posh, Mel C then Mel B (I'll get on to her shortly). Since as long as I can remember it had been my absolute dream to meet all five Spice Girls. So far, I've only managed to tick off Mel B and probably the less said about that the better. Oh OK, go on then, I'll tell you about that first.

Lorcan and I were at an Olympics party in 2012 the night before the closing ceremony when who should we see across the room but Mel B? We were telling everyone that Lorcan had won gold in the dressage that night and sidled up to Mel B who we would inform next of his success. Mel B was impressed. So impressed that she wanted to take this young horseman home to sunny LA with her. 'I LIKE YOU!' she shouted at him before asking for his email address equally loudly. I was given her phone and, in summary, I cocked up the email address. Lorcan is yet to join Mel B's gang. He maintains his life would be very different if only I could spell 'O'Donoghue'.

Anyway, that was Mel B and now THIS is Mel C . . . where were we? Right, so Mel C had agreed to an interview and, violent morning sickness or not, I was on my way. I'd interviewed LOADS of celebrities hungover in the past (soz, old boss) and this would be no different, surely?

The interview was fine. I asked her questions that *Smash Hits* had asked the Spice Girls in the nineties and she seemed to think it was fun and said something about Victoria Beckham which went on to be used by loads of other mags and newspapers. I was listening to her answers, but I was also thinking about her life as we talked. There are only a handful of people who can say they've reached their goals like a Spice Girl has. Professionally, she has experienced probably everything she ever dared dream of. There's not much they didn't do. She'd had her own Chuppa Chup lolly, ffs. She'd also gone on to have her daughter Scarlet so knew first-hand how that felt in terms of life events. But what had created the most happiness, I wondered? Living out your professional dreams or having a child?

After the interview, I told Mel C I was having a baby. I didn't bother filling her in on the situation – I didn't expect her to be interested. But I did ask her one thing: 'In terms of happiness, how does your career compare to your having your daughter?'

Without a second's thought, she said: 'Nothing ever compared to the feeling of having my daughter.'

I'd been hardwired to think happiness was sticking to the life plan formula of having a decent job, settling down then having children. Breaking the order would mean unhappiness. But for the first time, I thought – rather than being the thing to take everything away, this baby could make me happier than anything. Thank you, Mel C, you probably never realised how much you changed that scared pregnant girl's mindset that day.

True to say, that baby did make me happier than anything else. But a job like my old one – well, that wouldn't be bad either. The icing on the cake, you could say. But even if I were to host the Oscars one day (which I'm pretty sure I won't), being a mum to my son will still be the most important work I ever did. And I'm OK with that.

## P.S.

While that chapter ended, another one didn't and I wasn't the only one earning my keep in those early days. Young Frederick and his devilish good looks weren't going to be ignored for long and by the time he was four months old he snapped up his own modelling agent. The boy got more work than I did in twenty-eight years.

Baby modelling is, predictably, a mad old world. Like pretty much every parent whose baby gets into an agency, I had illusions – or more accurately delusions – that we'd make enough money to privately educate him for life and probably buy a house too. No such luck.

However, the back of his head did make it into a Nescafé advert once – the proceeds of which are waiting for him in his very own bank account for when he's older. At first, we had 'direct bookings' which were lovely instant 'jobs' where we'd be treated really nicely. For these, you don't have to go to a casting or audition – you are booked just off the back of your portfolio of pictures. On one of these there was even an on-hand nanny to look after the children on the set. On another we were given all the toys and play mats from the shoot to take home afterwards as well as our fee – which is a lot when you actually get the work. Alas, all that glitters is not gold.

We soon found out we'd just been lucky with those initial direct bookings and found that eighty per cent of the time you have to attend 'castings' before you get jobs like this and it was these that ended Fred's baby modelling career before it even really got started. 'Castings' would usually be held in a big studio space somewhere very far away from where we lived and the agent would give us £20 to get there and back. There would be a queue of about fifty other parents and babies waiting to meet the photographer, who would take about two photos which you were never allowed to see before moving on to the next one.

It was cut-throat stuff, a conveyor belt of tiny, dribbling humans unknowingly waiting for their big break. While queueing you'd pray that your darling Kate-Moss-in-waiting wouldn't be the one to have a meltdown or a poo just as they reached their (literally) two minutes in the spotlight. However, increasingly, my little Giselle was that very one. Plus, I started to feel increasingly angry on the shoots at how little anyone seems to respect the *ahem* tiny talent. The day a photographer sighed and said, 'I'm just waiting to get some pics where his eye is less wonky,' was the day we quit baby modelling.

And like this chapter, that was the end of that.

# 9

# GETTING BACK ON THE HORSE

I n many ways, I was chuffed to be doing the whole mum thing solo. I could give my wartorn vagina as much of a rest as I wanted, I could starfish in my own bed during the 0.00008 hours' sleep I was getting, etc. But the time came when I was ready to get back on the horse, so to speak, and start dating again. Like Carrie Bradshaw, if Carrie got knocked up, abandoned and moved back in with her parents in the home counties. Sequel, anyone?

I surmised that Tinder was for the hot and childless of which I considered myself neither, so decided to sign up to Match.com – which is basically where your divorced auntie would go to pull. A landscape of men in their fifties with usernames like 'NICEGUYHANK' or 'DALE1956' and lots of ':-)'. I was essentially one step away from the *Daily Mail* Blind Date page. Match.com gives you a more thorough dating CV than any app ever did and includes a section on children. Now I was in the 'already have' bracket rather than 'never' or 'someday'. I quickly discovered life isn't fruitful on Match.

com for the 'already have' bracket and, messages dwindling, I naïvely decided to leave it blank. Not lying as such, just careful truth editing. Life in the blank space category was far more productive than the 'already have' category and soon I was messaging back and forth with men who were also paying per month to find their soulmate.

After a few days I finally received a message from a man who was under fifty and looked sort of acceptable. I definitely *wouldn't* have thought so pre-baby, but I'd decided I was different now and standards had to be lowered accordingly. Don't worry, I definitely don't think this now – this was likely more of that temporary post-baby insanity. Around this time, I also grew my hair and dyed it a more 'natural' blonde colour – which was probably the first request in hairdressing history to look 'more like a mum'. So with my self-esteem hitting an all-time low, I accepted to go on a date with a primary school teacher who looked a bit like Duncan from Blue.

We'd been messaging for about a week, with no mention of significant tiny others, when he asked if I'd like to meet for a drink. First dates off the internet serve as a formality to ensure the person isn't actually a nymphomaniac/pervert/megalomaniac/narcissist/married man/catfish. Then, all being well, you can go for dinner for date two. Plus, no one wants to eat food in front of someone they've never met before (even Angelina Jolie doesn't look attractive chewing with her mouth open). Nervous eating is the only type of eating I don't enjoy. And so it came to be, my first post-baby date. To prepare myself I had a WKD in the bath at home getting ready, just to take the edge off.

Well, it is, of course, a truth universally acknowledged that first dates unhinge even the most together of people who didn't give birth four months previous. I felt the most nervous I think I've ever felt about anything, including childbirth. I hadn't been on a date in over a year and in between that I'd harvested a human being from my internal organs. And of course, there was also the spectacular dumping and subsequent abandonment thrown into the mix to really tinker with the old self-esteem.

Then I had to think what to wear. Oh, the woes of first-date clothing! I had been favouring pyjamas disguised as 'activewear' for the previous four months; I needed to up my game. The first-date costume must make one think of sex – but *not* that the wearer has had loads of it. The shoes must be high enough to suitably elongate the legs, but low enough to avoid emasculating a more diminutive date. And the dress? Well, I'm sure you're meant to choose something that shows off your figure but as I had just had a baby I opted for a dress that could double up as a tent if we got stranded on this date at any point. The thinking behind it was that the tent was a mask of illusion and it might fool my date into thinking that the body of Gisele might be lurking under there. So with my Dear Grylls-favoured frock on and tiny clutch bag filled with, er, nothing, I hit the pavement and walked into town to face the music of my first date in a LONG time. Since one became two.

First things first, he looked a lot less like Duncan from Blue in real life. Maybe Duncan from Blue if you saw him through a window smeared with Vaseline. He was definitely shorter than his profile had led me to believe (WHY IS THIS ALWAYS

A THING?) and had styled his hair into a spiky quiff like Simon from *The Inbetweeners* last seen IRL on boys at my Year 6 school disco. But there I was, doing my very best to charm him: excelling in all the necessary eyelash fluttering, laughing at his average jokes, saying 'wow' to his stories of life in the primary school fast lane. So yes, charm offensive. Or maybe just offensive, depending on how you look at it.

'Tell me something crazy about you . . .' he asked, to which my tired, date-shy baby brain did two things. First it had a sudden attack of Tourette's, then it said (not out loud, luckily):

'TELL HIM YOU'RE WEARING A WIG.'

'TELL HIM YOUR GRANDMOTHER'S IN PRISON UNDER THE TERRORISM ACT.'

'TELL HIM THAT BEFORE YOU PUT IN YOUR TAMPONS YOU DIP THEM IN CRÈME DE MENTHE.'

All before packing up for the day and going home leaving me to giggle girlishly (idiot) and say, 'Oh, I don't know! Sometimes when I'm hungover, I watch old *Newsnight* episodes to see what haircuts politicians had in the 1980s.' Great.

Looking back, I think I just wanted him to like me to validate that I still was datable, still fanciable and that I could still 'do' the whole men thing. In any case, I think my inane answer must have temporarily lowered my guard, because that, my friends, is when the shit bomb went off. He asked me who I was living with to which I said:

'Well, I'm back with my parents at the moment because I had my little boy not so long ago—'

'As in a baby?' he said.

'Yes, I suppose you could call him one of those. He's four months old.' The silence felt like it was pushing against me.

I appreciate now that a four-month-old baby is a very tiny, very new addition, but back then I felt like I was basically saying that I'd had him forever because four months is a long time in baby world. Plus, I'd been pregnant a LONG time so my time off the dating scene felt way longer than it probably seemed to this guy. I decided to just grin and hope he wanted to have sex with me enough to just brush over it for now.

'Do you not think you should have mentioned that on your profile?' he finally responded.

To which the 'me' of now says, 'Sorry hun, I don't really, no.' The 'me' of then was like, 'I suppose you are right. Sorry, I should have mentioned it. Is it a problem?'

It seemed it was a problem. He took a sharp intake of breath, actually clicked his knuckles, let out a sad sigh and said: 'I suppose not. It's not so much of a problem. I mean, we've all got skeletons in our closet. Take me for example; I've got Crohn's disease . . .'

Right there in the middle of the almost nice gastro pub, he compared my little son to living with a chronic illness. Now only I, and I alone, am allowed to take such a reductive viewpoint of parenting. I wish I could say now that I 'see where he was coming from' but I never will. Unbelievably, thinking I would now be rendered permanently hideous to all men, I was still keen to go out with sort-of Duncan from Blue again, and being so remarkably better looking than him, I expected him to feel the same. Although we only had one drink, he promised to 'give me a text' (don't they all? Sigh). Did he say goodbye or see you later? I was too drunk to care.

The next day I received what I thought was the 'day after' text. However, it read; 'Hi Amy, thanks for a good evening. You are obviously a great girl but I think we are looking for different things. Sorry.' Ideally, 'sorry' shouldn't be included in a post-date text message. 'Sorry' suggests you haven't exactly aced that round. I wished I'd drunk his on-the-house Limoncello. I had another WKD in the bath that night to drown my sorrows.

Being rejected by a man with funny ears after he'd compared my child to a debilitating illness wasn't ideal for my already rock-bottom self-confidence. But it taught me one thing: paying for Match.com didn't necessarily produce a match worth paying for, and so I went back to what I knew. I cut and bleached my hair and re-activated Tinder. Basing my love life around one line of text and a few pictures seemed a far more sensible option. This time round, I added in a picture of me with Freddy. Unlike most of the Tinder photos posed with random kids (all the better to show off one's 'softer side'), this had the benefit of actually being my child. I paid so little attention to the bio that it was a month before I noticed Lorcan had changed it to 'Gone Girl without the husband'. Which is perhaps testament to how little anyone pays attention to the writing on Tinder.

Turns out, Tinder was just as shit as when I had left it. Quickly, I established a pet hate for men who have pictures with children or babies and feel it necessary to point out 'DON'T WORRY, THE KID'S NOT MINE' – these are usually the same men who quote their height on the next line. Because that is what women want, right? Childless, very tall men? Also, if that kid really isn't yours then whose is it, please? Are all parties aware you are using said kid as a pawn in your grubby Tinder games? I have seriously considered changing my bio to '5 foot 4 inches. The kid is mine' just to make a point. Other reasons Tinder is a gross invention include: instant gratification, false bravado and short men lying about their height. I also absolutely could do without having to court pen friends via my smartphone in order to get to IRL date territory. Women, particularly busy mums, just don't have time for all that – even since the dawn of predictive text. Tinder in the home counties is even worse than London and basically the married, the unemployed and the ones who have moved back home 'for a bit' are the best a girl can get. The ones left on the shelf, essentially. Sorry, Berkhamsted, but it's true. I have been tempted to travel into central London and straight back again just for a decent swipe, much like the heyday of Pokémon Go.

After not-Duncan-from-Blue-gate, I quickly learned to cut the possible trauma of a 'big reveal' by mentioning I was a mum as early as I could. I don't mean I crowbarred it in, rather I would just slip it into the conversation. For instance, people on Tinder LOVE talking about weekend plans, don't they? So as soon as I received a message saying, 'Got much planned for the weekend?', I would say something like, 'Oh not much, just taking my little boy out.' That means they would then know, but it didn't come with a drum roll and a big dramatic pause. That's not to say I didn't get some highly inappropriate and douchebag responses from time to time, which actually did well to weed out the losers early on – a nice plus of dating *con bambino*. 'Btw I do appreciate you giving me "the nod" about the child early on' – that's the type of message that really got on my tits. I bet that same 'dude' would also have called my kid 'baggage'.

So it was much harder to find men who weren't certified idiots and understood the benefits of dating a single mum – such as, we have excellent snacks in our cupboards and will never have to stay over at your house and take up all the space in your bed. On the downside, this also means no morning sex and limited spooning.

However, even once I managed to find a bloke who wasn't a total ignoramus, actually getting on the date was the next obstacle I would face. Yep, when you have a kid there is way more to date preparation than just deciding whether to shave your legs past the knees and which pointlessly small clutch bag to take with you. Not that I ever had time to weigh up my accessory options anyway. Nope, I just tended to grab my normal bag, which always inevitably contained shedloads of baby stuff that I never had time to swap out. A pack of baby wipes, a Kinder Egg toy, a chewed crayon . . . Still, the latter did once come in useful when my phone had run out of battery – I was able to take down someone's number in crayon on a nappy.

Anyway, back to my point – PREPARATION. I was no longer just liaising with my date; oh no, now I also had to find one of my fellow responsible adults to watch my most prized possession while I was out. In fact, consider if you will that the lone mother will have to do this every single time they EVER wish to leave the house without their child. EVERY SINGLE TIME. Sixty per cent of the time my mum would be on hand to take over mothering duties while I was courting. However, since retiring, my parents also spent a large chunk of their time in Spain. Which was how I met the person who is both the nemesis and the saviour of the single mum – THE BABYSITTER.

Yes, babysitters grant freedom but AT WHAT PRICE? Essentially, this babysitting racket is daylight robbery. You pay £10 an hour for a teenager to watch your telly and eat all your food, while texting you things like 'I can't work out the remote' before silently judging you when you come in ever so slightly tipsy. And finding a decent one is pretty much impossible. One babysitter I used couldn't even put my child to bed so I came in to find him fast asleep on the sofa. Still, one doesn't want to die alone so forking out is a must. Plus, Freddy loves it because he can drink all the milk he wants, watch eighteen episodes of *PAW Patrol* and (probably) go to sleep very much not on time.

Now, I know what you are thinking – TEN WHOLE POUNDS AN HOUR? Allow me to explain. The first time I used a babysitter I asked her what she charged and she said she 'didn't mind'. This answer was cunning on her part as a) it sounds very polite and b) everyone knows no one likes a skinflint. So not wanting to seem really tight I just plucked £10 out the air and just like that – the rate was set. Sometimes I wonder if I could moonlight as a babysitter as it's such excellent business. Alas, then I'd have to find my own babysitter and so it would go on like some sort of weird babysitter *Inception*. Even though she's on premium rates, I feel bad asking her to bath him, so usually I bath him while I shave my legs in the water. Sometimes I'll share his bath to save time. I have even, on occasion, been known to take nudes in said bath. Yeah, mums take nudes too, OK? And frankly, I am time poor.

Because I decided that babysitters cost £10 an hour, I normally got my babysitter to come as late as possible so while I put my make-up on and do my hair, Freddy, in theory, played on the carpet next to me. In reality, he would grab EVERYTHING and throw it across the room. When he wasn't doing a make-up bag smash and grab, he would be burning things with the hairdryer. Or going through all my stuff, which is likely why I once found my beloved single gal essential – my Rabbit (of the rampant variety) – stuffed in his toy box. I think he mistook it for a Hatchimal. This is also probably why I never left the house feeling exactly as polished as I would like to.

All this cost and effort did have one advantage – it definitely made me pickier about who I went out with. Well, that is if I could find a date that hadn't already said something offensive about my child to go out with in the first place. And considering my rock-bottom low standards, I certainly needed some sort of filtering system. Saying that, a lot of the time, when push came to date, I quite often couldn't be bothered to go out anyway – often I arranged dates with all the best intentions only to cancel to stay in with one of those peel-off face masks and watch *Peep Show* in bed. Unless I'd booked a babysitter in which case I had to go due to the financial outlay. God forbid a date would cancel on the day, in which case you just lost the money and most likely spent the rest of the week looking into payday loans.

But the best thing for busy men about dating a single mum? Just like Cinderella, we have to be home by midnight. Dates with us are short, snappy, and great for men who have to be up early in the morning. Well, apart from one occasion when

I accidentally got more than tipsy and ended up rolling in at 4 a.m. The teenage extortionist wasn't sure whether to report me as a missing person. Getting up the next day was the least of all the fun. All of this meant that dates were fewer and further between and when they didn't go well, it was worse than before because it felt like more of an investment. And bad dates obviously still happened; only this time round I was paying £10 an hour to wonder how someone could seem SO different over WhatsApp.

So far, I have had to relate Freddy's conception circumstances on every single first date. Normally they try to coyly edge round the subject. However, curiosity eventually gets the better of them and they can't resist chucking in a 'Soooo . . . does Freddy see much of his dad?' To which I say no, and that opens up a whole can of worms rather instantly. Interestingly, blokes usually seem quietly relieved, as this means they'll never have to meet my ex. That's not to say they aren't generally emasculated by his existence and convinced I am still in love with him.

I did, on occasion, invite a date or two back to my house for a drink, meaning there was a moment where I had to introduce mystery Tinder man to my babysitter or, worse, my mum. And there were only so many times you could do that before the babysitter started asking questions. If it were my mum at home then the date would be the one with the questions. This was also normally the moment the whole 'me being a mum' thing would really hit home with the bloke folk. Generally, it was the first sighting of Freddy's toy box that made it all too real for some, and it would become an excellent way of separating the men from the boys. However, nothing ruins sexy sofa snogging ambience like the watchful eye of Daddy Pig. Not to mention the intermittent crackling of a baby monitor, or even worse an actual, crying, woken-up child. That normally has them 'calling it a night' and me darting upstairs quicker than you can say 'Coffee?'

What I found to be much more cost-effective was the lunch date – ideal for me because I'm freelance and Freddy's in nursery so no babysitter extortion was required. Although this did reduce the pool down to shift workers and the unemployed . . . And despite all this effort, it just seemed to be bad date after bad date. Three years of bad dates, to be exact. There was Aaron, who worked in recruitment and loved his BMW more than he would ever love me. Richard, the old uni fling who wore his swimming shorts to our date; Stuart, the guy who was REALLY not over being dumped the week before; and so the list went on. Jon was a typical example of how dates went back then.

Jon and I had the best first date after matching on Tinder. The chat was witty, easy and hilarious – the kind where you want people to overhear you because your conversation is so damn sparkling. We ended up very drunkenly snogging A LOT, singing TLC's 'No Scrubs' in a karaoke bar and going home far later than expected. He even paid for my Uber home from central London to Hertfordshire – which is a LOT of Uber. The next day we did the texting that ordinarily leads you to date two . . . but it just never happened. A week later, the messages dwindled and we never spoke again. Vitally, it was HIS turn to text, just in case you were wondering. Which did leave me convinced I must essentially be emotionally brain dead, having misinterpreted everything. Two weeks later, I received this text message: 'As much fun as the date was – and it was an absolute blast – I got the impression you wanted something more serious and were looking for a boyfriend. I'm just looking for fun whenever I'm in town. In hindsight I should have asked you instead of assuming you weren't into hooking up. Sorry.'

Everyone in the online dating world just seemed to want a hook up and all the blokes just saw you as one date in between their next swipe. My view from the frontline was that we'd become a nation of horny Tinder addicts craving matches and dating had become a game. We'd turned our phones into Gameboys but unlike those Italian plumbers we were REAL people with real feelings. Sorry, but didn't anyone just want to y'know, fall in LOVE any more? Instead, it seemed like a culture of racking and stacking had taken over from that soppy nonsense, which meant I just couldn't find anyone who I was on the same page with. I wasn't looking for much – just something more than a quick date and a shag.

Before I knew it, it had been one whole year and nine months that I had gone without sex. One year and nine months of absolutely zero how's yer father, hiding the salami – whatever your euphemism of choice may be. When it's not only been that long, but you've also pushed seven pounds of human out your bits in the meantime, you do get a little concerned that things might not be the same. You might have, er, forgotten how to 'do it'. Or, worse, your bits don't want to cooperate like they used to. By this stage, most girls have wisely invested in trusty husbands who have legally committed to put up with whatever vagina they have been left with.

The first time I had sex after having a baby is not one that I am proud of. For me, sex is the most powerful, most intimate, and most meaningful when I've got a connection with someone. Every other time, it's felt pointless. This time felt not only pointless but Poundland cheap.

It happened when Freddy was about eight months old. I had been doing everything humanly possible to combat 'looking like I'd had a baby' and had been spending a frankly insane two hours a day in the gym, terrified that my body had changed. I get that this probably isn't for everyone, but I was on a one-woman mission to sweat and ache like I'd never done before. I'd do an hour of HIIT followed by an hour of heavy weight-training most weekdays. As a result, I was quickly in the best shape of my life. That summer, I took Freddy to Spain with my parents, having taken 'No carbs before Marbs' VERY seriously indeed. While we were there, my friend Rume was also in the area with two friends I didn't know and they invited me to this totally Boujis daytime pool party. My parents agreed to babysit on the condition that I wouldn't get drunk and would be home by the evening. Well, I did get drunk and I wasn't home in the evening.

Anyone who has seen *TOWIE* in Marbella will be familiar with what this pool party was like. Think bikinis with wedges, body chains and blow dries and a pool not to swim in but to sort of stand and sway to monotonous house music in. Now this added to midday sun, low self-esteem and buckets of booze was never going to end well. I was hellbent on proving to everyone that despite the countless terrible dates, unexpected entry into motherhood and absence of the father of my child I was still desirable. I was no different to everyone else. The main problem, though, was that the only person I needed to convince was myself, because I was the only one that had a hang-up that no one wanted me. In fact, the girls I was away with were all single too and hating Tinder – the only difference was that they weren't mums.

I had run 6km every evening of the holiday just to be in shape at this party. My headspace fast became that of a teenage boy desperate to get rid of his virginity. While we were there, we met a group of (very) young football players and I started knocking back drinks like a sixteen-year-old at her first house party. Before long I was drunk and in fantasy land. Soon I was chatting to just one and I told him I'd been married and my husband had left me the day after the wedding. It was better than the truth and I revelled in his concern.

After the party ended, everyone spilled out into the night and somehow, this (very) young footballer and me were on the beach and before I knew it, we were having sex. I say before I knew it because I can hardly remember it. Everything suddenly seemed to merge into this one moment – the dumping, the pregnancy, the new life, the new body, Freddy, motherhood – and I burst out crying. Through tears and with the man still inside me I said: 'Do I feel normal?' Writing about this now still makes me flush with shame. So much that I was unsure whether to include this story but decided that in the name of honesty, I would. The way I was made single when I was pregnant had damaged me and subconsciously, I'd been trying to prove I was desirable ever since. It was actually seeing it through that brought me to the realisation that I didn't need to prove anything.

The next day I had to lie to my parents and take Freddy in his buggy with me to buy the morning-after pill. He missed an afternoon playing in the sand to be carted off to the pharmacy because his mother was such a liability. I was completely disgusted with myself. I waited for Freddy to fall asleep and then sat on a bench with a bottle of water, took the pill and cried. Cried because I was so irresponsible. Cried because this wasn't how mothers act. Cried because it wasn't how I wanted to act. I'm not judging any mums who do this type of thing on the reg – I'm just saying that while that might be YOU, it definitely wasn't me. I wasn't valuing myself and I saw sex and my body as the only way of getting attention. I tried for a while to convince myself it was all 'free love' and I was sexually liberated and fabulous. But I know how it made me feel, I know my motivations – and they were less than ideal. I was looking for approval via sex and trust me, you can look as hard as you want but there is no approval to be found there. And now I can never listen to the song 'Sex on the Beach' without being transported into a memory of weird, sobby sex with a nineteen-year-old footballer I'd only met two hours before.

Eventually, just after Freddy had turned one, I did actually manage to get myself a boyfriend. He was a dad to a seven-year-old girl so he 'got' the whole parenting thing. In those days, I saw him as gorgeous and delicious and everything I had been waiting to meet when I was blithely flailing around on Match. com all those months before. He was a definite step up from all the cretins that had been doing the internet dating rounds. I'd met this one after a mutual friend decided we would be a match and set us up on a date. He'd been through a divorce and before that, by the sounds of things, a pretty unsatisfying marriage (all very grown up – he was forty), so he reckoned we were totally on the same page.

We were both a bit out of practice. However, as it turns out, sex really is like riding a bike. The very best bike in the whole world that you wanted for ages and ages. THE BLOODY TOUR DE FRANCE. The only problem was I could rarely sleep over – only when I could leave Freddy with my mother – which meant an inevitable post-coital slump to my car and back to my house, which always made me feel a teeny bit like a call girl. Plus, there was the part-time issue. He didn't see things as being serious enough for me to meet his daughter so we only saw each other in the time he didn't have her, which was half the week. Freddy was so young then I was happy for the two to spend time together and I did always feel like I wanted something more serious whereas he was happy with things as they were. Basically, it was a 5:2 diet of a relationship.

Turns out lots of chemistry and not much else doesn't make for a long-term thing and it wasn't to last. While in the midst of our break-up, I ended up having one of the three one-night stands I have had in my life, all fuelled very much by alcohol-induced lapses in my already questionable judgement. The first was at university – all I remember was a tattoo of a dove on his ribs and I still can't look at the soap in the same way. The second of which, on the beach in Spain, you already know about.

As for the third, well, it's men like him and attitudes like his that had me so terrified, so convinced I would have a problem 'down there'. After this one, the man actually said; 'Wow, I was really worried because I know you've had a kid but . . . well, I'm impressed.' Champagne for my vagina! Not only did it serve as a door to the world, but it also still, shockingly, works OK — 'impressively' so, in fact. FYI, I didn't sleep with that man again. Following on from my two dabblings with promiscuity and the one previous at university I started to realise it wasn't for me and that it was shallow, superficial and unfulfilling. Monogamy or nothing, that's what I wanted. However, to get to this you have to go on 'dates' and most of these were frankly with idiots.

Another very disturbing incident, which I think shows the male obsession with the post-childbirth vagina nicely, happened when a man I was on a date with asked if I had a 'Harry Potter scar'. I'll just leave that there to sink in and move on, shall I? But if I did HAVE to add something, it would be that a worrying amount of men are WAY too interested in how breastfeeding works and whether you still are/could.

Some menfolk seem to assume that because I am a mum, which, yes, is pretty serious, I am looking for strictly serious relationships only, in other words that I want to draft them in ASAP to fill in the 'dad' role. This whole 'I think we are looking for different things' assumption first uttered to me by crap Duncan from Blue has stalked me throughout my whole single mum dating career. Sorry chaps, but I learned pretty quickly NOT to introduce blokes to Freddy too early. I definitely made that mistake pretty spectacularly . . .

When Freddy had just turned two, I experienced another bout of temporary insanity when I 'fell in love' with an old friend who I had previously had absolutely zero physical attraction to. With my standards getting increasingly lower by the day, I was so 'sure' of this connection that I let him meet Freddy

WAY too soon, and we even booked to take him on holiday for New Year. Obviously, Freddy got to know the man in question pretty well and when I awoke from my temporary insanity – prompted by this man asking me for 'spending money' to take on holiday with no intention of giving it back – Freddy wondered where he had gone. I think he missed him a bit. Well, he didn't know about the penchant for passive-aggressive arguments and unfortunate bicep to belly ratio did he?

Luckily, he will have no real memory of this but it provided me with an important realisation. I made a deal with myself to not trust my own mind, whatever it says, and I made a strict rule that no one meets Freddy. Well, they can meet him as 'Mummy's friend' but there would be no boyfriend-esque behaviour. I'd approach things as if we were in a public swimming pool – no kissing, no heavy petting and no dive-bombing – for at least six months.

Another of 'Mummy's friends' that didn't work out was a short-lived fling with a man called Ed. The problem with Ed was that he just could not get his pretty little head around the fact that I was a mum. In fact, I think he chose to bury that pretty little head in the sand. I'm still not sure what Ed found quite so terrifying about a two-year-old but whenever the pair did meet Ed would go very red indeed as if he'd just bumped into his ex at the family planning clinic. 'Hi, er, mate,' he'd say – limply holding his hand out for a high five that Freddy was too young to compute. I didn't understand his behaviour – until one day I met the source of his phobia.

Being another of those commitment-phobes I loved to court, Ed never let me meet his family. However, one day his auntie arrived at his flat unannounced, leaving him with no choice but to introduce us. Quickly, it became apparent that man came from a fairly conservative family. His auntie was very interested to hear about what the tattoo on my foot meant before quickly adding: 'Just don't you dare doing anything like that to yourself, will you Ed?' When she found out that I was a single mum – well, the tattoo paled into insignificance. The poor lady just couldn't understand the fact I had a child at twenty-four and was saddened by my 'plight'. Turns out Ed had been raised in a strict Catholic household where unmarried mothers wouldn't be the most welcome of additions. 'What on earth did your mother have to say when you came home and said you were pregnant?' she said, aghast. Well, as you know, my mum didn't say anything – she just involuntarily drove to Leicester instead. However, after that she said what you would expect to say to a self-sufficient 24-year-old living on her own: 'It's your decision.' It was hardly teenage pregnancy territory, after all.

Ed's aunt invited us to Scotland but we never made it. He broke up with me a couple of weeks later saying that although he 'had a great month' he 'couldn't see us long-term'. In his dumping speech he told me that he thought I was just 'too much', which got me thinking. Well, it wasn't the first time I'd been told as much. For a second (OK, more like a couple of days) I questioned how I could change and reset myself to the desired appropriate level. Then I thought, 'Fuck that.' I'm not 'too much' – they're not enough. It'd be pretty hard to dilute myself so I decided to continue in my quest to find someone who liked me, to quote Bridget Jones, 'just the way I am', which was apparently frothing off the boil.

People would tell me all the time that what I needed was a nice 'single dad', as he'd understand my parenting plight. Indeed, the playing field would be nice and level for once, which would surely be all my dreams come true. Plus, I could probably avoid going through childbirth again because he'd already have his own. But the thing about single dads is all they think you want to talk about (or is it all that they want to talk about?) is kids. Kids and circumstances ... It can quickly become a competition for who leads the least glamorous life and that wasn't really my bag. I like to imagine my life is quite glamorous at times, actually. Especially when I'm on a date, which in my head sees me starring in my very own Reese Witherspoon-esque romcom. Normally, I'm Julia Roberts in *Notting Hill*, just 'standing in front of a boy asking him to love her'.

Single dads are also normally divorced and have had this whole life before that I just can't relate to. That was the thing about being a NEVER MARRIED single mum; they're just single girls who happen to be mums. It's really that uncomplicated. In reality, it didn't matter whether they have zero kids or ten; I just wanted to find a bloke who rated Freddy and me as much as we do. That's all. It's just taking a little longer than I anticipated.

# 10

# YOU CAN'T SIT WITH US

I should probably start this chapter with a 'thank you' because without this lot my life would be a lot more lonely. I'm talking about friends. No, not *Friends* – although granted, those six have also got me through some dark times. But my friends, the ones who have been there from the blue-line right up until the writing of this sentence. Unlike any bloke, they stuck by me and subsequently Freddy. So to all my friends: I love you lot, you are awesome.

I love you despite most of you being on occasion spectacularly clueless when it comes to children. Well, I know as well as anyone that until you personally bear one, you don't really have much idea. 'But I look after my niece all the time!' I hear my former childless self say. Yeah, you did and you did an OK job, they didn't die, but now you know you need the full-on immersive experience to know the real ins and outs of the inexplicable, part-time delightful, part-time torturous but always surprising psychology of The Child. Because, wow, do those little guys keep you on your toes. Especially ones that belong to you – yikes, those really are the worst.

Here's a little story that sums up my beloved yet child-phobic mates. 'It's fine for kids – it's got a garden' reads a typical message. That's what childless people think children need – pub gardens. If Trip Advisor says there's a garden then it'll be FINE. The kids will love it and we can stay ALL night. I never want to be one of those people who is like 'Oh, you have no idea until you have kids, we must go to soft play instead', so I go along with it. (Even though I have recently noticed a trend for hipster ball pits that keep popping up all over East London – so actually, maybe soft play wouldn't be such a bad idea?) On every single occasion, I find myself thinking that *this* time, this could be the one pub garden in London which is actually for children and might even have a slide or a monkey bar or two. Alas, no, and we arrive to what would have been a garden before it was jam-packed full of fairy lights, benches, hipsters and vapes. Now instead it resembles an al fresco Urban Outfitters. Actually, is that a sand pit? Oh wait, it's an ashtray.

Still, we persevere and squeeze onto a shared table with a load of other twentysomethings for whom the closest they have ever come to a baby is that Clear Blue advert you can't skip on YouTube. My friend comes back to the group from the bar with two drinks, undoubtedly Aperol Spritzes. She sees then two-year-old Freddy, picks him up like a sports bag, plonks him on the floor behind us and sits in his place before trying to pick up on the conversation. Well, it was never going to be straightforward being the first by about ten years to pop out a baby and I'm sure that if one of them was the one in the nursing bra I would have probably done the same. Well, maybe without all the plonking. But it's frustrating having to 'go first' sometimes.

One time when Freddy was about six months old four (very childless) friends from my old life and I decided to plan a group trip to Center Parcs. I loved this because it showed they were trying so hard to accommodate us. I doubt very much that they wanted to go to Center Parcs but they did it for us. We were sorting out how many bedrooms we would need when my friend Becky made the following suggestion: 'Couldn't Freddy's crib just go in the bathroom?' In a bid to save space, Freddy was momentarily consigned to the damp, dark, communal washroom. When a person is tiny, immobile and can't speak for themselves, those unfamiliar with them definitely think they are more like little pets than little people. I remember thinking as much of my little nephews, finding all three totally nonsensical and really, well, boring until they were walking and talking. I quite possibly found dogs more entertaining than small babies, especially the extra boring newborn ones. So I didn't blame my pals for being clueless; I would have been exactly the same before I landed my own 24/7 child to give me a crash course in all things baby.

When Freddy was born, my friends were beyond incredible. Even when I was pregnant, they were amazing. They rallied round, bringing all kinds of presents but most importantly themselves. They even threw me a surprise baby shower that we posted to Facebook under the album name B.S., carefully concealing my bump and any baby paraphernalia in all the pictures so that the people I hadn't told would be none the wiser. My friend Rume bought me a multipack of twenty-four plain white Primark scratch mittens. She didn't know what they were but 'apparently babies need them'. All twenty-four of them. I also received lots of clothes for four-year-olds because someone somewhere said that 'babies grow fast'. As well as several 'Good Luck' cards because no one knew what the hell card people buy for baby showers. Well, you can't buy new baby cards without an actual baby, can you? Plus the logic defo made sense because I needed all the luck I could get.

I think that these friends just couldn't believe what was happening any more than me. They knew me as the girl who always got too drunk and got the taxi driver to let them smoke fags out the window – I was probably the last on the list of people who would pack herself off to give birth in Hertford-shire. But once they knew my decision no one questioned it and instantly they threw themselves into stocking me up with all the bibs and scratch mittens Primark had to offer. They also really love Fred. Despite them thinking his crib would be fine in the bathroom. Remember, right at the beginning none us really knew what to do with the little meatball, and I didn't have much clearer ideas about the whole thing than they did. Which made for some very hilarious first meetings. Why can NO ONE 'get' the whole newborn wobbly head thing? Maybe they should start teaching us that in PSHE.

Being the first in our group to bust life from between my legs did make me the parenting guinea pig. I know that the childless HATE it when they are accused of such ignorance but it's only when you have a kid you realise how little you knew. Lorcan and my friend Talia babysat for me once when Freddy was two (TWO being proper human age where they eat meals and drink water and squash, things like that) and when I came back he had drunk five bottles of milk. In the day. They said they thought babies could just have as much milk as they wanted. I blame *Rugrats*.

A lot of my old friends also seem to assume that since having a baby I ducked out of working and instead just watch loads of daytime telly and walk around Primark. Mate, that was called maternity leave. However, I also think that's just what anyone thinks about people who don't work in an office. What I think they sometimes forget is that they have their evenings to themselves without the relentlessness of the bath, story and bedtime routine. Which is why, my friends, I sometimes am not quite as vocal in the nightly WhatsApp debates about Kylie Jenner's baby name as I might have been before. It can be a right old head-scratcher how to be involved in a life that feels so dramatically different from yours but please, don't stop talking to me about that shit – I love it. I hate talking about immunisations and Mr fucking Tumble (asshole) – so do me a favour and keep on sending it through. When I'm tucked up in bed catching up on it all late at night, it's my happy place.

But when I do see my mates sometimes it can be a bit of a struggle to switch off my 'mum' brain as much as I will myself to do so. Please excuse my social awkwardness; I've been at home with a toddler all day. It's like when you haven't spoken all morning and you are worried your dodgy throat will make you sound like an old dog attempting to bark. And if you catch me talking about my kid all the time PLEASE call me out – I remember people like that and I don't want to be one of those boring assholes.

Conventionally, I was supposed to become bitter and annoyed that none of them had the foggiest how to change a nappy and my friends were supposed to become bored and judgemental of me droning on about Tommy Tippee. But it would be too simplistic to say 'we didn't have anything in common any more' after I gave birth because we still have loads. It's just the mum stuff they don't get. But there's a lot more to life than mum stuff – there is RuPaul, there's who's judging Porn Idol at G-A-Y late that week, there's Liam Payne and Cheryl – don't worry, there is still loads to talk about when you live vicariously through celebrities and social media like us. Plus, I'm a journalist – I can edit to make the baby stuff sort of interesting, surely? Everyone loves to see how an electric breast pump actually works. I hope I know my audience. I can inform them of what babies are really like and they can be as shocked and grossed out as I was the first time I learned all this stuff. I am reporting live from the frontline of motherhood for all my friends' entertainment. My strategy is to keep it light and avoid scrolling through hundreds of essentially the same photo – yes, fascinating to me but to my mates, possibly not so much.

It would be wrong to say that the day I became a mum I didn't lose friends, and much of the signatures in those Good Luck cards I haven't seen since I was pregnant. But the ones left are definitely the cream of the crop and the only ones I need. They were there at the hospital with champagne the day Freddy was born, they bought him a hundred hilariously unnecessary Christmas presents and are the most fleeky aunties and uncles a baby could hope for. My friend Carl recently bought Freddy an exact replica of his Adidas jacket and tiny little Vans so that they could twin. Unconfirmed reports suggest he may have done it for the Insta likes. To celebrate the most unlikely of babysitting troops we started having 'Freddy's Christmas Lunch' every year where we all have a party in Fred's honour and celebrate him as if he were the baby Jesus himself. The first of these was when Freddy was just three months old and it's happened the last weekend before Christmas ever since.

What I really want my childless friends to know is that I appreciate them and I wish I could spend more time with them. To my friends – I miss you and that's why I hold on to you a little bit too long when I hug you to say hello when we meet. I WANT to meet up more, but I told the babysitter I'd pay her £10 an hour and I have no money. It's either that or bring a toddler on a train which I'll tell you now is the ninth circle of hell. I'm sorry I'm always late when we meet up – children really do make everything take ages. They never have both shoes and need the goddamn toilet more than your grandmother. Packing to go out with a kid is like packing to go on a holiday to an unknown destination – you must plan for all eventualities. Then most of the time you end up using none of it and just thinking how very heavy it is.

But thank you for your patience, even when I don't remember birthdays as well as I used to. I know that you know I am the same person I always have been but sometimes I worry you think I've ditched you for my new life. It's not that at all, it's just there aren't enough hours in the day. I wish the government would arrange some extra ones here and there – like when you are clubbing the night the clocks go back and it's just THE BEST THING. But instead, having a kid is like the morning the clocks go forward, every morning. My iPhone MUST be lying, alas no, I really am just this knackered.

However, my friends, there are a few things I would ask of you. Please don't text me at 6 p.m. on a Friday saying 'Fancy Friday drinks?' and then following it up with 'Just get a babysitter!' as if that is the easiest thing in the world. IF YOU'D SAID IN ADVANCE I PROBABLY COULD HAVE COME. Children are leeches of spontaneity. I'm not asking for much – just a couple of days, even ONE DAY to up my chances of actually being able to come instead of watching it all on Instagram Story. As Freddy gets older, he gets more low-maintenance and babysitters are easier to find, but please just bear in mind I need a little time to arrange one. Also, please know just how envious I am when you lot pop off for weekends here and there because that is one thing I know I can only get away with doing about once or twice a year, and that's if I'm lucky. I don't want to go backpacking around South East Asia but I really would like to come to Manchester or Brighton when you go.

Equally know that I am happy. I know that you probably worried from the moment I decided I would let nature take its course and I know I moan about living all the way over in Berkhamsted and vow to move back to London every time I get PMT but really . . . I'm happy. You can park wherever you want here and Freddy loves being near his grandparents and goes to an awesome nursery. So it's all good, honestly. But when I see pictures of you all out doing something without me, it does hurt a teeny bit. FOMO sucks. And sometimes a tiny, evil part of my brain does think, 'How can they have that much fun without me?' and then I get paranoid and feel redundant – like I've lost my importance in the group. But it will be just at that moment when Lorcan will message and suggest he comes to see us all the way from East London and his flatmates who definitely aren't as cool as me and I'm reminded that he is thinking of us and maybe even misses us a teeny bit like we miss him.

And for Lorcan, my BFF always and forever – I want you to know that you are still and always will be a priority in my life – even if I did once stand you up because I fell asleep during Freddy's nap. You called me dumb that day. I was dumb. But think of my baby like a new, really important hobby. I've still got time to care about your promotion at work and your latest Tinder date. In fact, I live for that shit – it's my other hobby, hearing about you. Yeah, life changes but like the Spice Girls taught me, FRIENDSHIP NEVER ENDS. My favourite times are when Lorcan comes over to Berkhamsted to stay the night with us. We put Freddy to bed and then watch all the crap we used to watch on telly and it's like nothing ever changed at all. Well, until we are disrupted by the milk Führer's demands for refills. But when it comes to friendships, ours hasn't changed. If anything, going through everything together from the finding out to the birth to now has made us even closer. We still laugh at the same stuff, watch the same telly and talk about the same people. We do the exact same shit we used to do before there was a tiny sleeping human in the other room.

One of my biggest fears after giving birth was having my identity taken away from me. Would my friends still see me in the same way now I also was firm friends – well, more like frenemies – with Iggle Piggle? I know for a fact there is a WhatsApp group in existence for organising nights out that I am not a part of. But then, why would I be? I go out essentially twice a year now. And even then I just moan when people ask me to dance. But that's the main thing I miss – seeing my friends. Because since Freddy was born, I don't see them as much as I would like. Distance plays a factor; their hangovers play another. Unfortunately, the best time for me and Freddy is Sunday afternoons – we make plans with the best intentions, but I have been bailed on enough times to know that quite often Saturday night gets the better of my mates. Our lifestyles aren't as compatible as they used to be but that doesn't mean we as people aren't. Plus, I have managed to make time to properly go away minus child a few times.

Secret Garden Party festival this year very nearly killed this (very knackered) mum, but it was still very awesome indeed. It might have rained (and OH did it pour) basically the entire time and was an utter sludgy mud fest – honestly it was like being in the centre of a melting chocolate egg – but I had the best weekend I could have hoped for. No dashing off on the last train anticipating the hell that is morning-after childcare. Plus, it was amazing being with my friends who I don't see enough now I'm a mum. I hadn't laughed so much for months; I swear my tummy is still achy however many months later. Even though just writing that makes me feel a bit guilty because Freddy wasn't there. But breaks are important. As much as I love being a mum, I also love being just another 28-year-old every so often. So while my festival raving might be more of an annual occasion nowadays and my hangovers ten times more killer, the party didn't end the second my waters broke.

However, festivals, friends and Freddy can also be VERY compatible. Despite my concerns it could be an extended version of the times we have spent in London's 'family pub gardens', Freddy had the time of his darn life at Standon Calling festival. The family area there is AMAZING – mainly because I was doing some of the children's entertaining but I shan't brag . . . The baby rave was IN-TENTS (little camping joke there). As it turned out, Fred was an absolute festival natural; he was a dream in the tent and he could run around, be as loud and generally uncivilised as he wanted and basically release his inner lunatic without any complaints. We found our happy place with festivals – something that we could all enjoy together (finally) – and not a vape-filled pub garden in sight.

But as much as I love my childless mates, I knew it would be nice to have some friends who don't call a muslin square a 'Muslim square'. Luckily motherhood gave me a new best friend who knew about all things baby. There was nothing I couldn't ask her and she always found me exactly what I needed – we were so close that sometimes she even finished my sentences. Although, come to think of it, she was awfully uptight about spelling. But best of all she was always there just when I needed her – even at 3 a.m.

We met just after I fell pregnant and have been attached ever since. Our relationship was Wi-Fi dependent but it was fine because we have a very strong connection. Yes, like so many new mums – and who are we kidding, humans in general – the internet was my new best friend. Actually, as a bit of a hypochondriac, we'd always had a mild flirtation. But motherhood ramped our relationship to the next level.

Even stuff I know that I know I just pop in the search engine – just to, y'know, check. Well, you can never ask the baby if you did that right, so you ask the internet instead. It's like your mum, only less judgemental and available twenty-four hours a day. Plus, the internet is way easier than a book and you can do it with one hand while feeding. And when you get bored of baby stuff, you can go on ASOS. At which point you may well also go off on weird, wired, late-night tangents that start with Kegel exercises and end with the purchase of a wholly pointless bath seat that swivels 180 degrees. Or you may have gone off the subject of babies altogether and are now balls deep in a Wikipedia page about every single Big Brother contestant. Unlimited, free knowledge – Matilda would have had a bloody field day. We've all been there, hun. But it's 3 a.m., put down the iPad and go to sleep already, you lunatic.

In my case, my single status meant I moved back to my hometown – somewhere I hadn't lived since I was eighteen – to have some help from my own mum. Living at home, let's talk about that for a sec, shall we? Moving to Hertfordshire felt like I'd been evacuated to the countryside double in size, clutching a pregnancy pillow, a Moses basket and a feeling of imminent doom. I felt like I'd been reduced to age sixteen once again, hankering for a lock on my bedroom door. Becoming a parent is usually something that makes you feel VERY grown up but for me, when combined with moving back to the family home, I felt more like the baby than the mother.

When Freddy had just learned to walk he left the cosy womb of Shelley's childminding and graduated on to the local nursery. My reasoning behind this decision was that now he was mobile he would probably like to cruise around and have his pick of mini pals and also get used to an environment similar to school before he eventually started there. Shelley's was perfect for him when he was a baby but now I felt like he could do with the extra kids and extra space. This also meant lots and lots of other mums, of whom I was terrified.

In the early days, when I went to pick Freddy up from nursery, I became a caricature in my head. I turned into Katie Price in a My Little Pony jumper and imagined I had nothing at all in common with anyone. This probably wasn't the case, but for ages I felt like being unmarried and living at home with my parents meant I stuck out like the sore thumb variety. Or Katie Price at a public school gate. I pretended for a long time that I wasn't bothered – I didn't want 'mum' friends as I'd just find them boring, anyway. All Laura Ashley picnic rugs and husbands with Ralph Lauren cable knits.

I convinced myself for a while that it wasn't about me – it was them. I had the edge on these mum types because I was the (probably) only one among them who could actually meet and go out with Tom Hardy. Well, in theory. Even though I had actually already met him and was yet to go out with him. Oh and actually, isn't he married? But basically, they were all coupled up whereas who knew what handsome man lay ahead for me? Even more basically, I was on the market and they were (probably) well jel. I told myself this to make myself feel OK about not being able to make any mum friends. Looking back, how would they have even known I was a single mum? They were all on their own too. But I felt like I was a marked woman and everyone knew my sordid little secret. On the occasion I would pick up my child at the same time as another mum, I would agonise my way through the conversation, praying I was smiling and nodding at the same time as we exchanged small talk about our very different family lives. I willed myself to be natural but just felt so out of my depth.

I hadn't lived in my hometown since I was eighteen and so returning made me paranoid about being 'different'. Mums were grown up – while they were speeding through the life stage levels with husbands, mortgages and plans of 'baby number two', I'd been held back a year ticking the 'living at home with parents' box. I might have been a parent, but I never felt more useless or less independent. Even though I KNEW it was only temporary, moving home felt like the biggest stamp of failure yet. I felt on a different level to what I regarded as 'proper' mums and convinced I couldn't fit in with them even if I tried to. As long as my mum was making my dinner, I felt like I would be considered a joke to these 'proper' families. This is really why I didn't go to NCT classes, because I didn't feel I could be considered on the same level as these women. It didn't help that the town my parents live in is Yummy Mummy central with a very well-stocked Waitrose.

Feeling like this, I was convinced I would be greeted by a sea of well-heeled couples at Freddy's nursery summer picnic. I spotted one mum that I'd already noticed sometimes when I was picking Freddy up. She had the Range Rover, she had the Boden skirt, so I concluded she had the husband. Our two boys, it transpired, had become best friends with each other. Ugh, trust Freddy to make friends with the heir of the future head of the PTA. She introduced herself to me and I concluded that her husband must be parking the car or something. 'Would you like a glass of Prosecco?' she said. Prosecco? At a nursery picnic? Maybe we did have more in common than I first thought. 'Er, yes please'.

She took me over to her picnic rug – which was indeed Laura Ashley – on which was sat her sister and their mum. No blokes. Her husband must be at work, I thought. They're probably one of those couples who say they 'pass like ships in the night' because they just work so hard and have so much money. As we got talking, though, it soon transpired I'd got it all wrong. She wasn't a smug married mum; she wasn't even married, she was one of me. I quickly realised that being so obsessed with the idea that people were judging me had perhaps made me the most judgemental of all. Her name was Becky and after she'd got married she'd moved to New Zealand with her husband and they'd had their son. They'd since split, however, and he had stayed behind for his job. So here she was, back living with her mum – a single mum to Freddy's pal. Minus the Boden skirt and Range Rover, she was just like me.

I started seeing more and more of Becky and it was perfect because the boys were such good friends. It was such a bloody joy to find someone who understood the single mum balancing act so perfectly. Unlike my childless friends, she knew what it was like to have a human plus one. And unlike my coupled-up friends with kids, she knew what it was like to be trying to salvage a social life and romantic life alongside being a mother. She also knew what it was like to be pushing thirty and living in your mum's walk-in wardrobe. Even though her stint was far more short-lived than mine she had been a very successful PR and had managed to buy a very lovely house to match her very lovely skirt and very lovely car.

Making friends with Becky taught me the importance of having total common ground with at least one person in your life. You don't have to be lifelong friends – you just have to be able to share the same experiences at that same time. Situational soulmates, if you like. Because it's through friends like this that you can find a new normal. When you're amongst people in a similar situation you are suddenly no longer an outcast or a failure. Where no one else will understand, they will. I cursed myself for not seeing the light sooner.

By chance, I had also reconnected with people I'd been friends with as a teenager who still lived locally. I saw a girl who I had gone to many a gig with as a two-belt-wearing back-combed emo kid teenager post on MySpace that she had just had a baby and after commenting on each other's posts here and there we met up. Yeah, she was a mum but first and foremost she was my teenage buddy so it all felt way less threatening. Plus, I was pretty sure that like me she didn't quite get where Boden even exists – is it online? As it turned out, she had her baby Amelia on my birthday, which is five days before Freddy was born. She was married by now but knew all about being a single mum from her experiences with her older daughter Kara, who was seven.

Laura and the girls fast became Fred's and mine's go-to pals. We saw so much of each other that we said it would probably make sense to buy one big house and all live in it together.

By the time we said this, Laura was actually going through a divorce from Millie's dad so actually it probably should have really happened. We go to Center Parcs as a dysfunctional little family and Millie comes to us for sleepovers and Freddy goes to Millie's. They are like cousins rather than friends. And sometimes I think Laura has become more like a sister for me. It's perfect because Freddy has two instant pals to play with, Laura and I can endure the hell that is soft play together and we can swipe Tinder while we are there too. We can even go speed dating afterwards, if the babysitter is free. Plus, with no family commitments and debilitating hangovers unlikely, Laura and her girls, like us, tend to have their weekends free.

I also fast appreciated that mums weren't boring. I took Lorcan to an all-mums event and he said they were on par with gays for a good night out. Basically, don't generalise. I did and that was really dumb. I did because I was scared of rejection. I was so worried about what people were thinking of my situation that I painted all the other family circumstances with one brush. However, scratch beneath the surface and you quickly see that no situation is the same. Every parental set-up, every family is as unique as mine. Plus, everyone is so busy trying to get their kid into nursery and not miss their train it's very unlikely they are even giving me a second thought.

Remember when I said I felt like I had to dress a certain way after I had a baby? Now I can't stand anyone who says they didn't fit in because they don't 'dress like a mum'. That's like saying all women dress the same. Excuse me while I blow your brain but some mums are trendy, and some mums are conservative dressers. They are all different. I fast became known as the 'scruffy mum', as I work mainly from home and rock up mainly in a gym kit or a tracksuit. This is probably why, for a long time, Freddy's nursery assumed I was unemployed. I got that out of one of the junior staff I used as a babysitter once. Feeling like an unwashed slob also put me off making pals off the bat. At the beginning, I did struggle. But my attitude was all wrong. I'd decided I wouldn't fit in before I'd even tried to. So this mindset was never going to be much of a mum friend magnet.

Nursery gatherings and birthday parties still scare the crap out of me, though. Although I no longer feel like I've snuck in uninvited, I still get hella intimidated by big groups of mums I don't know. Especially the glam mums who are always perfectly made up even at 9 a.m. and step out of a Range Rover. I bet that Glam Mum has a super-important job in the city – almost definitely a lawyer or banker. Something that involves chic pencil skirts. Why dress up for the nursery run, I reason, until I see Glam Mum and resolve to make more of an effort tomorrow. Well until it actually gets to tomorrow morning and in the rush to do breakfast, brush teeth and find the other white sock I realise I can't be bothered. Glam Mum would probably do the same if she worked from home.

I do like well-connected mum though – because she's the one who knows everything about everyone and can help me sniff out my fellow solo mamas. And of course, what's not to like about the mum who makes the AMAZING cakes – yeah, she's a show-off but WOW are they delicious. However, before you ask she doesn't take commissions because that would just 'take the fun out of it'. Then there is intimidatingly organized mum who has a STRICT RSVP on their kid's party invitation.

I KNOW everyone is busy – but some people do busy better than others and I'm just not great at it. And finally, good old getting divorced mum who you've noticed has been looking a little out of sorts for a while now. I want to remind her that probably half the class will be in her shoes by the time we reach senior school so chin up.

If you are struggling to make mum pals IRL then apps like Mush are amazing. I was asked to try it out for a newspaper article and at first, I had my reservations. It sounded like Tinder for mums and that just felt a bit too weird for me. Especially as, unlike most of the mums on there, I was also on real Tinder. God forbid I got the apps confused and started unknowingly chatting up a mummy match. However, Kate Middleton has even said how fab it is so I decided it was worth giving a chance.

At first, it did feel a bit strange to be messaging random mums and making sure to toe the line between friendly and creepy, and sometimes I found myself running out of things to say. Luckily, I ended up connecting with a girl called Lucy. She's around my age and has a little boy of one and we got on really quickly. It wasn't long before we moved things over to WhatsApp and when things got to the stage of voice notes I asked if she'd like to come over for a playdate. It was so refreshing to have someone to talk to who just 'got' what I was on about when it came to my life. I don't want to talk about babies all the time but for someone to already have the context was amazing. I felt like I'd found a real gem – thank you to Mush.

However, a meeting that came out of a group on Facebook didn't go as well. You see, every so often you meet a mum who learns that you are single and she grins and tells you, 'OMG I totally know what you mean – my husband is literally ALWAYS working.' This chick was very much this. She also went on to try and sell me Herbalife. I find it very hard to trust anyone selling Herbalife. Now let's discuss the phenomenon of 'married single mums', a.k.a. married women whose partners go away for work sometimes. There is a new tendency across mummy blogs and websites to run articles entitled: 'X Ways You Are a Married Single Mum'. Er, just a sec. He's working away to make your family money, right? Your kid will be very much OK with the fact his Dad is away and he is coming back. When your kid has just pushed you beyond the brink, you don't have to be the one who bears the entire force of nuclear, mega tantrum. All the time. You'll never get the pity looks and heads cocked in sympathy by well-meaning smug marrieds. While you may live in our shoes for a period of time, you get to take them off. So you are NOT 'just like a single mum'.

What I quickly learned was that making mum friends is just like making any other type of friends. Some people you will click with almost immediately, others burn more slowly and some, well, you can't get on with everyone, can you? But life as a mum is brighter and better when you surround yourself with awesome people. There is a mama friend out there for every type of mum, you just have to look in the right places. And if we ever meet, know that I might be smiling on the outside, but I'm a paranoid wreck on the inside and just want you to like me. So why not come over and say hi? I think I'd quite like that.

# 11

# THIS MUM CAN JUGGLE

**B**eing a single parent, I am responsible for everything. Making sure that my kid is clean and alive, making sure I'm clean and alive, making sure that the house is livable, that there is more than a lump of cheese and a can of Fanta in the fridge, that I have childcare, that I am (sort of) sticking to a budget – every single aspect of parenthood is on my shoulders. And while I expected to be kind of crap at 'doing it all', somehow I managed. Sure, I've learned to cut corners where I can but – just like when I crammed the night before every exam I've ever done – I got good results in the end. I might approach 'doing it all' in just about the most lax way you can but I think I'm doing OK. I think that *we* are doing OK. Even though I probably won't ever have a pedicure again and I've resigned myself to box-dyeing my hair, overall parenthood has never been about 'sacrifice' – it's been about the best fun I've ever had. However, I have had to learn to spin all the plates and have had a few smash along the way.

When I found out I was pregnant, I thought: 'My body can't possibly fit all that lot in, and as for my vagina? No chance.' But then miraculously, my body DID accommodate that baby and it did manage to come out ... eventually. Not without some minor hiccups along the way. In the same way, I thought my life can't possibly fit this in – it's full enough as it is, thanks – but miraculously again, it did. Likewise not without some minor hiccups along the way. But when the new baby dust settled and the transition into parenthood was complete, I somehow did figure out a way to live a happy, well-rounded life. Turns out it's not something that exclusively belongs to childless people. That's not to say it isn't a bit of a juggling act and occasionally we drop all the balls. But I quickly learned that I could do SO much more than I ever imagined because I HAD to. And once the baby arrived, it became less about having to and more about wanting to because the squish made it all worth it. Even the home-dyed hair.

What's more, it is SO satisfying to know that I can and I have done it all by myself. We somehow do what people with two wages do with just one. I hope this is also a good role model for Freddy – he can see what a person can achieve single-handedly.

I've had to learn to cram my entire adult life into the hours of nursery and when he is asleep. At first, I had the respite of nap times but since he turned three these have come to an end, so now it's just nursery hours and after bedtime. So anything that isn't motherhood-related needs to be squeezed into this window. Which is why sometimes I toy with the idea of a 6 p.m. bedtime and why I now understand why my own mother was so absolutely insane about getting us to bed 'on time'.

Obviously, some things we can share – we love going to the supermarket together and he even helps unload the dishwasher now he's a bit older – but I just have to bear in mind that everything, and I mean everything, takes double the time when you have a miniature accomplice tagging along. Shopping can go awry when Freddy does his favourite activity – running through rails of clothes and pulling the lot clean off. And to anyone who thinks I could take him to places like my hairdresser's or to get my nails done then you clearly haven't met a toddler. Either that or you get off on civil unrest. However, when he was tiny I did used to take him to the leg waxers – which presumably made for some mother-and-son bonding memories he will cherish forever. I used to go for a manicure every two weeks. Now, well, I cut my nails with a Swiss Army knife.

Basically, motherhood straps you for time. I feel this no more strongly than when I glance at the clock and midday has turned into 5.10 p.m. and I have to leave to collect Freddy from nursery having very much not finished what I was doing. And no one likes doing anything vaguely work-related after 8 p.m., do they? I have to fit in at least one hour of awful telly per day to save me from certain insanity. So I've got more efficient in my task management. But where there has been efficiency there also has been the feeling that I am spreading myself a bit thin. I've had to get used to feeling like I'm treading water with my work – there's always more I wish I could have done. I have a list of things and ideas that I want to do about as long as Milton Keynes shopping centre. The longest in the world, would you believe. I finish tasks and generally meet my deadlines but I always feel like 'If ONLY I had more time . . .' then it could have been something special. I basically spend my work life chastising myself that things could have been better. This is only going to get worse when school starts – when my curfew moves to 3 p.m. But let's save that bit of woe for the future. On the plus side, it will be cheaper so swings and roundabouts.

'But can't you just work and put Freddy in front of CBeebies?' I hear the childless say. No. Because if I do that he needs something every five minutes, or he is hitting the keys on my laptop, or shutting the screen. I know that because it is what is happening right now. It's a Sunday and he's 'watching *Hop*' – you know, the Easter movie with Russell Brand as the voice of the bunny? – by which I mean he'll watch it for ten minutes and then he needs the toilet/says he's hungry/starts saying 'MUMMY TALK TO ME' which descends into jabbing the keyboard until he gets my attention.

This feeling that time just isn't cutting it isn't helped by the fact that small children love to move your shit around. Nothing says 'Have I got dementia?' like losing your keys for the billionth time only to eventually prise it out of your kid that he's hidden them 'in his truck'. That's a good twenty minutes you'll not be getting back. At the time of writing, four of my credit cards have been taken out of my purse; the theft has been admitted to but he 'can't remember' where he put them (N.B. I found them that evening in my underwear drawer). 'Well, why were you leaving your purse around, you mad woman?' I hear you say. Aha, no, you see these small children – they are cunning. Freddy's latest thing is to wheel his little truck over to things you've put out of his reach and use it as a crane of sorts to manoeuvre him to the level he requires. And the kid moves quickly: you are only ever one toilet break away from your next theft.

Nowadays, I also forget a lot of shit. When your mind is trying to think of a bazillion things at once the odd thing tends to get left behind. Generally, this is something that is at the top of my shopping list. Normally, milk. Despite now being three, Freddy still guzzles a LOT of milk – he just bloody loves the stuff. But while he is single-handedly propping up the dairy industry, I struggle to keep up with him. And when you are on your own, there is no popping out after nightfall. I've tried to improvise with almond milk but this was met with great disgust. And don't even think about watering down the teeny drip of milk I do have – it goes down like own-brand versions of Nutella.

And then there are perils of childcare, of which none is guaranteed. Once I had finally miraculously sourced the unicorn that was worry-free childcare, I was introduced to its hamartia, its fatal flaw. One of my previous jobs was collating the weekly 'Street Chic' feature for the *Metro* newspaper. You probably remember it if you ever pick up a *Metro*. People normally call it 'the page with all the girls on it?' – and yes, reductively speaking, it is that. But they were all wearing supposedly super-fashion-able clothes. My job was to trawl the streets of London with a photographer on the hunt to find girls to feature and then interview them about what they were wearing. Sounds easy enough until you factor in that they have to all be wearing clothes from one particular trend. For example, we would do a page of trench coats, or everyone would have to be wearing floral. Pulitzer is in the post, I am sure.

One week, I remember, we were doing horizontal stripes. Three weeks later we did vertical stripes. What fast became clear was that it's actually a bit tricky to think of a trend for every week and expect to find fifteen girls actually wearing it (we'd always take five extras so the editor could pick the best ten). But my job was to do just that. So my photographer Daniel and I would go stomping around London on the hunt for whatever we picked that week. Marl grey was a particularly desperate day. Parka jackets was a particularly rainy day: options were limited, shall we say. I think one week we actually just did 'scarves'. Every week I'd also have to write a short introduction on why that particular thing was trendy, which always included lots of words like 'perennial' and calling ugly colours pretty names like orange 'marsala' or yellow 'mustard'.

So on this particular week, we had just snapped horizontal stripes (*'Get ready to earn your style stripes with a perennial fashion favourite'*) number five when my phone rang:

'Hi, it's Janet here from the day nursery. We've just taken Freddy's temperature and it's 37.2.' My first thought is MY BABY, MY POOR BURNING-UP BABY. My second thought is 'Er, normal is 37, right?' But Janet continued: 'He's not really himself so we're asking you to come and pick him up.'

Er, sorry, what now? Don't I pay you people to look after him? If we DO have to come there then you better all be wearing horizontal fucking stripes because this is the only way we are going to sort this out. I'm sorry, I was angry. Angry and on a really tight deadline.

'Sorry, I'm in London working but I can be there in a couple of hours . . .?'

Just forty-five more minutes here and I'd be done and on the train.

'I'm sorry but it goes against our policy to have him here with a high temperature.'

They'd dropped the 'p' word and my hands were very much tied. There was nothing I could do or say, no one else I could send, so that was it – back to Berkhamsted ASAP for 0.2 of a degree. Work deadline was very much missed because ol' Junior Pants was home sick from school. Street Chic survived that week – but only because we had fur stoles on the back burner. *Cosy and super chic, wrap up with a faux fur stole this January.* The lesson I learned here was ALWAYS be well in advance with your plans and deadlines because you never know when that temperature might creep up 0.2 of a degree. And I also learned the hard way to be careful what you say to nursery. Just mentioning that your son brought back up some milk can have you quarantined at home for two days. I get it, of course; they have a duty of care, and I would be pissed off if Freddy came home sick because of something he'd caught there. Hell, I AM really pissed off when he turns up with a cold on what seems like a fortnightly basis. Is it just Freddy's nursery or are all of them essentially toddler flu camps?

Work commitments lie on eggshells when your kid is at nursery – which is why it's always ideal to have back-up. Luckily, my dear mother will normally swoop in to take over looking after Freddy and stuff him with chicken soup when I can't. But if not, it's important to have contingency plans or, at least, understanding bosses.

I haven't always had understanding bosses, however. This year I was working at a newspaper when the Beast from the East (remember when ALL the snow fell?) struck and closed Freddy's nursery. Mother on holiday; too short notice for the £10 an hour babysitter. I emailed my boss to tell her I wouldn't be able to make it in. She replied saying that she'd checked and that the trains *were* running and if I didn't come in then I wouldn't be asked to do any other shifts ever again. I had no choice but to write back saying, 'I'm sorry that you've set me such an ultimatum. Best wishes for the future.' Journalism really can be cut-throat when an editor considers staff replaceable and I lost a good strand of income that day.

Not mastering the balancing act like this has led to some bleak times that have momentarily overshadowed the awesomeness which is being a mum. There have been times I have thought, 'What have I done? I never needed to do this,' but it's only ever been fleeting. It's easy to use motherhood as something to blame when other areas of my life aren't going well. But using motherhood as a punching bag doesn't get me anywhere. Freddy just means things, people and life have to be more flexible and overall, they are.

And then there are the occasions when I am ill. Which must be fought against at ALL costs – because if I go down, well then we really are fucked. From that first incident with mastitis after Freddy was born, I knew getting ill would never be the sort of weird indulgence it once was. Getting ill used to mean the best (but often, yeah, also intermittently gross and unpleasant) excuse to not think about anything but getting better and watching the entire ten seasons of *Sex and the City* while people brought me things. I had glandular fever when I was sixteen and it was horrific but also oddly relaxing to be suspended from the world until further notice.

Now, with a child on your watch 24/7, there is no world suspension possible. If you are ill you have to just get on with it – while begging people to babysit. Normally, I can find someone to babysit for a window within the day while I drown myself in manuka honey and phlegm. But ultimately, in sickness and in health, that little blighter is my responsibility. When the extreme has happened and I have found myself with no one to look after him, I adopt the same tactics as hungover child-care and we play a lot of 'OK, I'll be the baby and you be the mummy'. However, me being ill also means I become obsessed with thinking 'WHAT IF HE CATCHES IT?' Because tandem illness is just beyond comprehension. TOUCH WOOD it is yet to strike us, but wow, does it set the fear of God within me. So far, the universe hasn't dared to be so cruel. I know that if it did happen though, I would have to put Freddy above myself, because that's what parenting is, isn't it? Prioritising someone ahead of yourself, always and forever. And when you feel beyond rough, those are the hardest times to resist being selfish.

Some people say that single parents have to learn to be a mum and a dad – that they play both roles. But I'm not so sure about that. I'm definitely a mum but I'm not sure I have the five o'clock shadow to be a dad too. I suppose what they are thinking is that single mums have to be the breadwinners *and* the nurturers – we have to be able to work to make enough money to give our children good lives while also being available for them as much as possible. In that sense, I guess I am a mum and a dad.

Even more basic than that, it's true I have taken a job that is normally shared by two people. Single mums have to be every role a parent plays – which means we have to be everything from the disciplinarian to the loving, coochie-coo nurturer. A lot of single-parent critics argue that it is impossible for one person to play two roles. Obviously, these people have never seen Lindsay Lohan in *The Parent Trap*. Plus, if *Inside Out* taught me anything, it's that the best things are a combination. Even better, things you totally wouldn't put together are often the *best* combinations. Jam and cheese sandwiches, McDonald's chips and milkshake (don't knock it till you've tried it). I just had to learn to be both the chips and the milkshake.

If you say that ONLY women can be the nurturers and ONLY men can be disciplinarians and that's why we need the male and female roles then we run on to stony ground probably only welcome during a phone-in with Nick Ferrari. Surely that is just seriously limiting both genders, not to mention same-sex parents. This is appealing to nothing but stereotypes best left in an episode of *Mad Men*. The idea that women emote and behave strictly one way and men another is, in my opinion, b.s. Especially coming from a family in which my mother very much wore the trousers and my dad was the easy touch who I longed to accompany me to Tammy Girl because he just couldn't say no and I'd end up with the biggest haul that my mum would NEVER have said yes to. Both men and women are capable of explaining periods, playing football, teaching respect, scolding and praising – to say any of these lie with just one gender is just old-fashioned nonsense. When people talk about 'traditional roles', they are just describing personality traits that could be attached to mothers OR fathers. The family type that is best for children is one that has responsible, committed, stable parenting. If you can get two parents who can do this then yeah, it's probably better than one, but one really good parent can also be better than two crappy ones.

My personality type means I struggle with discipline – so yes, I conform to my feminine stereotype but that doesn't mean every mum does. Sheryl Sandberg is a single mum – you don't see her struggling to be taken seriously, do you? I'm just not a natural when it comes to discipline and historically, children tend not to take me too seriously. I volunteered in a primary school during sixth form and by day two the kids were calling me 'Mrs Nipples' and one even kicked me in the shin. The problem is I like to think I'm mates with the kids – so basically, I'd rather just NOT have to tell them off. But when you actually have your own kid, you realise that you have to become familiar with your strict side or things will crumble into certain Sodom and Gomorrah very quickly. Children can smell weakness and if you are too soft, you'll suffer and they will walk all over you – and in turn they will suffer, turning into children destined only for *Brat Camp*. I know this because Freddy has a tendency to particularly perform just for me. The problem is that Fred is like the Borg on *Star Trek* – once I've mastered how to deal with one thing he moves to a new frequency. It used to be not sleeping through, then it was hair-pulling, now it's tantrums. Meaning it's a constant learning curve. And lots of rewatching the *The Three-Day Nanny* on YouTube.

However, I do find comfort in knowing that most kids mug off their mums or whoever might be their primary care giver.

Every day, the nursery staff give me a little round up of what's gone on during the day – from activities to what he ate at meal times. They reckon he ate all his cucumber, played nicely and didn't pinch when he didn't get his way. Nah, that must be some other kid you're on about. Because on my watch, he is the child whose nickname is 'Beezle-bubby'.

But why ARE kids so different with their primary care givers? Apparently, it's because they just feel so darn SAFE with us. We've created a rod for our own backs by being nice to them. Nope, we really can't win, can we? They are hardwired to mug us off. They know that their mothers love them so much that they can ultimately get away with anything. Whereas when they are with other people the outcome is less predictable. Toddler logic says don't mess with strangers, save it all up for mum. However, just to make anyone currently suffering feel a bit better – apparently this stuff needs to happen to make emotionally intelligent, civilised beings of the future. The worse he is for me, the better he will be for society.

So when the child says 'no' to everything – EVERYTHING, even stuff he secretly wants to say yes to; when he says he 'can't' say please; when he tells me to 'stop talking NOW, Mummy'; when he pushes away full plates of food THAT I'VE JUST MADE and says he's had 'too many food'; when the only thing he will eat for breakfast is pasta and cheese, I just remind myself – the worse the tantrum now, the better the adult will be. Think of it like conservation or recycling.

For now the advice is DO NOT GIVE IN, indeed DO NOT NEGOTIATE with your tiny terrorist. Apparently you shouldn't raise your voice; you must stay calm and stick to your guns. I tried this out during a particularly heated conflict about him wanting to take our entire household supply of toilet rolls into his bedroom so he could 'line them up' and after twenty excruciating minutes my three-year-old gave in. He suddenly dropped the act and morphed back to his normal self. Five minutes after that he LAUGHED at the toilet roll meltdown. So it does work – eventually.

But when tantrums happen and you are a single parent there is no one to turn to for back-up, meaning that tantrums normally last longer than they would if there were two of us at the helm of the ship. Admittedly, discipline would probably be easier if I could share it with someone. On the plus side, I do have the freedom to totally decide the way to do this on my own and don't have to compromise on the best way to do things. But it's frightening as shit that I am solely responsible if things go tits up. And I know that if anything, however teeny, ever does go awry in his life then I will blame myself, because who else is there to blame?

When I was in about Year Five I remember doing my maths homework and confidently handing it in KNOWING I had got the lot right. It came back and I had got two out of ten correct. I had totally cocked it up. What if this is the same and I'm getting it all SO wrong? In this weird, slightly long-winded allegorical sense, yeah, it would be nice to share responsibility with someone. Similarly, there is a relentlessness in motherhood that can take its toll. It is, in fact, the most invisible, undervalued job going. There's no appraisal or comments section to give me feedback so it would probably be a relief to share the ups and the downs with someone who could reassure me on how I'm doing. I sometimes wish I had the knowledge whether I am just rubbish or actually the task is harder than it seems. Because when you are on your own, you lose that perspective.

However, saying that I have 'no one to share my worries with' because I am a single parent is just wrong. I share my worries with anyone who will listen – including you, right now. My mum is my main port of call – which, in my experience, isn't unusual for single mums and probably why so many of us live with our parents at the beginning. In fact, my own parents have been the ones who have really helped me manage to juggle everything since I became a mother. They have been a second-in-command since the day we arrived back from the hospital.

Now we have moved around the corner from my parents, Freddy still sees them most days. But they've always been there as a safety net for when things have got a little difficult. They've been there to babysit for me whether it was for work or a crap date and they've been there to moan to about it afterward. And although my dad did teach Freddy to say 'Yuck – pink is for girls' (which is not ideal but we're working on it) and does have a penchant for feeding him endless barbecued sausages, without him I would have been stuck too many times to count. The hours he's given up to step in to take Freddy to or from the nursery at the last minute – I would say with no complaints but that would be a lie – they're too many to mention. He was truly there when I needed him.

Single parents need support – luckily, I've got it. My parents help me discipline, they tell Freddy to stop pulling Mummy's hair but, most importantly, my mum has been my emotional crutch through all of this. People say that single mums miss out because they 'don't have anyone to share their thoughts with at the end of the day' – well, I know that I always have my mum. All mums know the importance of grandparents for their children but I think us single mums depend on them even more. You'd think being an unpaid servant for eighteen years plus preceded only by the horrors of childbirth would have put my mum off having more than one baby. Instead, she did it three times over, the nutter. And now she doesn't just look after us three; she looks after our kids too. For this she deserves a truckload of compensatory flowers, a personal serenade from Michael Buble and all other mum-friendly entertainers (see also Michael Ball and Alfie Boe) and personal exclusive use of Champneys until further notice. And my dad can have his Twiglets indefinitely served on an extra large white plate by Liz Hurley (his fave). He's very specific about the white plate; he says he can 'see them better' when they are on one of those.

I also have my pals to help me keep those balls in the air. Everyone says all singletons, single mums included, are lonely. Well, I wasn't a lonely singleton – so I wasn't going to be a lonely single mum. Birth didn't evaporate my social circle. Anyone who hasn't got a partner on hand to talk to just needs more WhatsApp groups in their lives. My childless friends might not always get what I'm on about but they will listen – which is much like a husband in many ways, I imagine. You just need PEOPLE to offload to and whether you are romantically involved with them or not, if you ask me, isn't massively relevant. There is Lovehoney for the rest.

While I don't share my parenting with anyone, I do share my problems or fears with a team of good supportive listeners

– even though Lorcan has admitted recently, 'Sometimes you do go on, but for those bits I just tune out.' But the point is he's always there to tune in when I need someone. So I have a brilliant support team in place: I go through my bills with my dad, I moan to my mum, and I go on holidays with friends.

That's not to say Freddy and I don't go away on our own sometimes and BLOODY LOVE IT. Just recently, we booked a cheap January weekend in Center Parcs, just the two of us, and had all the fun. We were the only double act – but who cares? Everyone probably just thought 'Dad' was off parking the car all weekend. And then when we weren't having all the fun I could plonk him in the crèche and go to the spa. Also, by the by, Virgin Holidays last year announced they were introducing tailored single-parent family prices for their holidays in the Caribbean – a recognition from Richy B that families come in all shapes and sizes, and that family ticket prices should reflect this.

I do totally understand that not all single parents have this supportive network, though. Luckily, I know some awesome people who can help you out with that: Gingerbread. I first came across the charity when they retweeted an article that I wrote (thanks, guys). They've been supporting single parents like me since 1918 and if you are feeling lonely or isolated they run Gingerbread groups all around the country where you can meet other parents in the same boat. They even have online forums – and, as anyone who has catfished their way through single pregnancy on Tinder will know, sometimes it is really comforting to just chat to someone via your laptop. Plus, if no one else gets it, then this lot will. And who knows, you might strike lucky with a single dad? Winky smiley implied.

That's another ball that was recently chucked in to juggle – I found a boyfriend. When Freddy was about two, I met the man whose Swiss Army knife I would use to give myself home pedicures with. When we met, I'd switched off dating. In fact, I'd had an epiphany of sorts. After two years of horrendous dating, I had stopped looking for new relationships and decided to enjoy the ones I had. I was so preoccupied with relentless dating, swiping, back-and-forth bullshit with strangers I was (rather foolishly) neglecting the real relationships I already had.

Eventually I realised what a mistake that was. Our society is obsessed with romantic relationships. They are prioritised above all others, regardless of the fact that we enjoy countless types of meaningful connections with other people. When I thought about it, it seemed an outdated social construction that you are somehow incomplete if you are single. The important thing is love and if you have enough of that in your life then you are winning. I had Freddy, my rather great and almost always hilarious friends and my impossibly patient and under-standing family. And finally, for the first time in as long as I remember, I realised those relationships were enough. I didn't need to look for anything because nothing was missing; I had all the love I needed in front of me already. Any more would just be a bonus ball.

And that's when I got my bonus ball. I truly believe that to have a successful romantic relationship you can't expect them to be your whole cake, just the icing. Enter Oliver, a man who seems to find me and Freddy as awesome as we do. He looks fab in swimming shorts and he can ski. He would look great on your arm at a Mother's Day lunch, but also all your friends would fancy him and wonder how you pulled him – a rare combo. He says he tried to chat me up in our local pub months before and that I gave him the brush off. Now, I remember this and that is not what happened. I assumed he was the type of chap who was making his way round the bar trying his luck with all the girls and I was just one of many. Plus, I thought that being a single mum with shrunken boobs, I probably wasn't too high up in the pecking order that night. It took me getting extremely drunk weeks later to finally ask him if he wanted to go out for lunch.

I hate it when people say 'whirlwind' but this really was. My friend Lauren says you have to count my life in dog years. What other people take seven years to do, I do in one. This could be said for my relationship with Oliver. Well, when you have a child things get serious quite quickly whether you like it or not. For a while I tried to deny this, as I had previously vowed never to even introduce Freddy to a new flame before six months. But I had found someone who made me so happy I felt like I had the Instagram love filter on permanently. Before I met Oliver I'd never felt real love before. I'd felt infatuation, I'd felt lust . . . but romantic love? Nah. He asks me how, then, I know I love him, and I tell him that Freddy taught me what love is and though it's different, the underlying current is the same. So I thought I could probably make an exception to the six-month rule in this case. Well, I'd made so many plans I'd never kept over the years that I decided to let my heart overrule my head now. I decided to introduce them.

Hell-bent on making an excellent first impression, I willed Freddy to be his best self to finally meet Oliver – but as he is a toddler, things were naturally catastrophically unpredictable. Though hardly surprising: Freddy hadn't exactly been on board with the change in numbers from the start. For him, three was definitely a crowd. When Olly was present, he'd shout 'NO' to everything, throw the newspapers clean off the coffee table, prompting the individual pages to fly up in the air, and at one point he even went to spit on the floor. It was like he'd just landed a part in *Green Street*.

Later, after he'd finally gone to bed, Oliver said: 'Freddy, he is a bit . . . naughty sometimes', and as many times as I protest 'He's not normally like this!' through a gritted grin, the more it seems like of course, that's what I'm going to say. Only he *really* isn't; he's a good, charming, lovely, gentle boy 99 per cent of the time (the remaining 1 per cent being tantrum time) but the idea of me having a second man taking my attention wheeled out his inner football hooligan for all to see. He'd morph into the worst jealous boyfriend, clingy and attention-seeking – if he were my latest squeeze and not my son he would be getting the elbow ASAP. But it's par for the course, I guess. He has had my undivided attention since the day his godfather cut that umbilical cord and his life started as a twosome – Mummy and Freddy. He probably doesn't want anyone else disrupting our all-he's-ever-known family set-up.

So Freddy didn't want Olly and I couldn't shake the thought that Olly didn't want Freddy. The same shameful, horrid, minus-a-million-mum-points – and just human points in general – thought invades my brain whenever I consider the future: 'He'd prefer me if I wasn't a mum.' I convince myself he thinks my son is an added extra that he'd rather didn't exist. Writing that sentence makes me feel like I've eaten dodgy curry as the pure guilt rises up inside me. To clarify, he's never suggested anything of the sort and this conclusion is nothing but a product of my very mad, overthinking brain. But I'm always conscious of the fact that he's landed himself with an instant child by staying with me.

It's settled over time, but it wasn't easy and often I felt like it wasn't fair on any of us involved. Now Olly and Freddy are proper pals, no chucking a single thing. Olly's misspent youth rollerblading has come in particularly useful and now their favourite thing to do currently is go to the skate park together on Saturdays. But it took me a LONG time to accept that my childless boyfriend would ever be able to see my perfect boy like I do.

Once, quite early on in our relationship, with this thought drilling away in my brain, I brought it up with him. He looked at me and within a second said: 'I'm not going to say I love Freddy because I don't know him yet, but I love you, and you are who you are because of him. If you didn't have Freddy, you wouldn't be you.' I couldn't have anticipated a more perfect answer; it hadn't even been in my list of possibilities. Now all I need to do is trust it's true.

So now I have the boyfriend, the job, the child and the friends and everything SOMEHOW seems to be coming up Milhouse. I feel like I am close to mastering the juggling act, to having it 'all'. Well, as much of it 'all' that is possible. I did an interview with Drew Barrymore once and asked her the age-old question you ask all celebrity mums – never dads, but that's a debate for another time – 'Can women have it all?' She said, 'I think we need to redefine the meaning of "all".' I agree. We can't have it all ALL the time but why does that have to be a bad thing? I believe 'having it all' and being a successful juggler should be judged by happiness. If you are happy in your situation, then you have it all.

I think children make people more positive, in general. Maybe it's the cuteness. The cuteness that can override any tantrum eventually, however nuclear. I can be having the worst day, but then I pick Freddy up from nursery, give him a cuddle and that day is turned around. There isn't a day he hasn't made me smile since he was born. And that's what keeps things balanced and the balls up in the air.

# 12

# WHERE'S MY DADDY?

It doesn't take a biology genius to work out that, ultimately, it takes two people to make a baby and somewhere along the line our numbers were diminished to just one. While I can try to give Freddy everything myself, I can't magic him up a dad. So when people say that children NEED one, of course I get offended, I get upset, I get touchy. Because whatever I do, I can't rustle up one of those. While I parent solo, biologically there are two people involved. I suppose this is the part where I am expected to say how bereft we are about our minimised family but if you've made it this far then you'll know that we are actually doing OK. So far, so good. But Freddy's only three, and the world is kinder and easier when you are three. Plus, it's hard to miss something you've never had. But I know the future holds questions that, right now, I'm not sure I know the answer to.

When you ring the doorbell at Freddy's nursery, every child in the class thinks that it's their turn to be picked up, prompting

Confessions of a Single Mum

them all to chant 'MY Mummy?', 'MY Daddy?' until it is revealed whose parent has arrived. This was how Freddy first picked up on the fact that there are mummies and this other weird thing called 'daddies' and they aren't just consigned to books and *Peppa Pig*. One day when he was about two, I was picking Freddy up when a small boy called Bertie looked at me quizzically and asked: 'Where's *Freddy's* daddy?' Aha, momentarily stumped by a two-and-a-half-year-old. This was the first time I'd ever been asked a question like this by someone I couldn't just say the truth to and, just as I'd feared, I felt like I was under a magnifying glass. However, I had my answer – I'd had it since I was pregnant – and now was the time to finally road test it.

'Well, you see, when Freddy was born he had just a mummy, no daddy. But he has a grandad and a nanny and lots of aunties and uncles.' The little boy registered the information and accepted it with a grin before going back to eating Play-Doh. I wish more people were like this little boy, but alas, not many are. Although it's definitely getting better, single-parent families are still considered 'worse off' than traditional families by most people. It seems we have a societal preoccupation with the idea that fathering is critical to churning out well-rounded members of society.

They might frustrate me now but I don't blame people for their automatic assumptions. Growing up, I expected to have a baby with a man and live happily ever after. I was hardwired, mainly by Disney, to think that's what little girls want and need – a prince. Or a Ken. It never occurred to me that Ken or Prince Charming could just abort the mission. Finding myself left in a family where my prince/Ken had hit the ejector seat automatically resigned me to feeling 'worse off' – and in turn I believed my son would surely suffer. Well, what a load of horse crap that was. Of course, a kid with two parents who are both responsible, nurturing, loving and involved with them all living under one roof has landed the best-case scenario and hit the family jackpot. But nowadays, that's about as much of a fairytale as all that Disney bullshit I delighted in so much as a little girl. Being one dad down isn't all bad, I promise you. Like everything in life, things come with pros and cons. Even good stuff has negatives: Disneyland has too many queues; ice cream makes you fat; long hot baths leave you prune-like. On the flip side, nothing is all bad – airplane toilets always have really nice hand cream, Kanye West has Kim Kardashian.

On the crap side, Freddy will one day realise that you *need* two people to make a baby and however much his mum, his grandparents, his aunties and uncles love him, he'll figure out that someone, somewhere along the line, decided that he'd rather not. And in that moment, we both lost something. I can give him the sun, the moon and the stars' worth of love but I can't fill in that gap. While he won't miss what he's never had, it would be naïve to say that there isn't something missing.

The day Freddy's biological dad decided to bugger off, I was terrified by the supposed burden I had placed on my child. I felt like I had shortchanged my baby by bringing him into the world in such circumstances. I felt guilt for robbing him of a parent and leaving him with just one.

I still can't get inside the truth of why Barry opted out of his life. I can only imagine he was just terrified and so, of course, I wonder if he regrets his decision now. But as shit as it was,

I can (sort of, almost, kind of) empathise with why Barry left, and I think Freddy will too. We weren't young, but we WERE immature and neither of our lives at that time lent themselves to the idea that a baby could slot in. The only time either of us was interested in kids was when they were on *Britain's Got Talent*. Barry never actually saw me pregnant, he never saw an actual baby, so for him, perhaps, it all just remained an idea – an idea that he was just too scared to face. I never wanted to force him to be a father, so while two loving and nurturing parents are obviously the Tesco Finest of family set-ups, we were never going to be a couple so the ending was never going to be straightforward for us. Therefore I can (sort of, almost, kind of) imagine how confusing it must all have been for him.

I like to think that I am sure he didn't make his decision lightly and that he agonised over what was the right thing to do. I suppose we just have a different idea of what right and wrong is. But that was his decision – and my decision is to do the very best bloody job I can to make sure that child that we both made is doing OK. And so far, he really is doing just that. So I don't have anything to blame Barry for – actually, I only have something to thank him for. Because he gave me the best thing: my son.

Just as he asked, I've never sent Barry a photo or tried to communicate with him; I didn't even let him know when Freddy was born. If Barry had wanted to be involved, I would have snapped up his offer and 100 per cent acknowledged a shared ownership situation. Once the baby had exited the confines of my womb, it would have been no more mine than his. I know that seems simple to say now – but I also know in my heart that, as hard as it inevitably would have been, I would have had to share, and to respect that a child has two biological parents. However, I do also know this creates its own difficulties and that, as a result, often the problem isn't so much absent fathers but access issues. I have two brothers going through it now, and it's truly awful.

In my case, though, Barry simply disappeared, so that's what we are dealing with – a man who willingly, willfully and intentionally chooses to remain absent. I have heard zero from him since he made that phone call to my dad when Freddy was two weeks old. It could make me feel sad that Barry's never tried to contact us but actually it makes me feel relieved. Relieved that we've managed this far without any disruption. It's being around conflict that causes trouble for kids and so far we've experienced nothing of the sort. I actually kind of respect how Barry has managed to stick to his guns. I suppose that's worthy of some weird credit. Although a bit of cash here and there would probably have been nice/useful. But really, it could have been a lot worse. It would have been so damaging for Freddy's biological dad to just be swanning in and out every so often – or, even worse, suddenly making a grand comeback after zero contact and expecting an instant relationship. Mate, Freddy and I went through TEETHING together, no amount of Saturday Pizza Hut trips will make up for that.

Very occasionally, I wonder what our lives would be like if Barry had stuck around to know his son. He would, like I have, the privilege of knowing a truly awesome kid – and even better, being able to say that he made him. Clear winner for him. But for Freddy and me, I think things would inevitably have been more complicated. Since Freddy was born, his life has been very straightforward – there has been no passing back and forth, no disruption to his life. His roots are clear and his home life uncomplicated and as a result he's such a happy boy who is getting more confident every day. Having a dad and a mum who live separately might have made things blurry, harder to make sense of. That said, at the same time, it's all he would have ever known – a mummy and a daddy who have separate houses, separate families and separate positives and negatives. So maybe it would have been fine.

On down days, I can't help but think a dad would have added more relationships and more love for Freddy. However, I also know that a negative relationship with his dad would have been worse than nothing at all. The thought that a father – any father – is better than none is just plain wrong. He could have been harsh or critical and had an impact that could have been far worse than just leaving a gap that we could fill with everyone else who loves us. But it would be foolish to the max not to assume that interruption and disruption COULD still lie ahead. Though I think it's unlikely: I don't yet have a definitive answer, but I think Barry made his decision that day and it was permanent – just like mine was when I walked out of that Marie Stopes clinic. However, I know more than anyone that you really don't know what you will do in certain situations until you are in them yourself. Sometimes you can surprise yourself as much as Louis Walsh in an *X Factor* deadlock. So who knows what the future holds?

I very rarely wonder if Barry thinks about the family that he could have had but will now never have. I used to think more about all that he was missing out on but now I just think that *he* was then and *we* are now. Unless time travel becomes a thing, he's already missed too much to expect to slot back in. I do sometimes think about the paternal grandparents who also have never made any contact with us – but equally my parents are easily worth all four. And Freddy is lucky because it's not all children who share such an incredible bond with their grandparents as Freddy does. Freddy might have only two grandparents instead of four, but they are almost as close to him as I am.

I also wonder if Barry's gone on to have any other children – because technically that would mean Freddy has biological brothers or sisters. It would mean that someone calls Barry's parents 'Nanny' and 'Grandad'. Will they know about Freddy? Will they want to know him? Will Freddy want to know them? I have A LOT of questions that currently I just don't and can't know the answers to. The truth is that I have no idea what goes through Barry's or his parents' heads when it comes to us.

However, if Freddy wants to try and contact Barry then that is a different story entirely. Excruciating as it is for me, I know I need to leave the door open as much as I want to slam it shut. I've watched enough *Long Lost Family* to know that he could be curious as to where he came from. I was also once rather unceremoniously grilled by Nicky Campbell on BBC Radio 5Live on this very subject, which got me thinking about all the possible futures rather than just the one I hope for. While I think one way, it's possible that Freddy might think otherwise. I promise you now, Nicky Campbell, I will never, ever lie to Freddy. I love my son more than I have ever disliked the actions of his biological dad – so although I won't encourage it, I will support his curiosity and never be selfish and stand in the way of it.

I know that for some people genes play an important role in learning their own identity and I will understand if my son asks to see pictures or know what type of person the man who contributed half his DNA is/was like. It will take all my stage-school acting skills, but I will do my utmost to only remember the good bits when I tell him his real origins. However, I am cautious of creating any possibility of hero worship or romanticising what Barry was like, so it'll be a careful balance to strike. But I never want to sound bitter or critical when I explain what happened to Freddy and I want him to know that he can always express his feelings truthfully to me, even if he thinks they might upset me. If he's sad about what happened, I want to know. If he's just pretty meh about the whole situation, I want to know that too.

My suspicion and hope is that he'll be too occupied with all the relationships he does have to spend time wallowing about the one he missed out on. But if that's not the case, I'm going to try hard not to take it personally. Easier said than done, I'm sure. I know that he will ask questions and I know that they will likely break my heart, but the best thing I can do is just answer them honestly. I'll have to fight every fibre in my body to stop me from being defensive. I know I have to try and not make it a taboo subject and keep things as light-hearted as possible. Freddy is a kid, and so he will treat the information however I give it out. If I'm awkward and overly serious then he'll think there is something to worry about. He needs to know that his dad didn't duck out because of anything he did and if I don't fill in the blanks he could draw his own conclusions.

I still see his dad every day when I look in Freddy's eyes. They are carbon copies of that Kit Harington glance that I was just so obsessed with. Those are an excellent genetic steal, if ever there was one. He is also starting to show a real talent for ball games, just like his biological genes did. But really, so far, that's where it ends. His personality, developing every day, just seems unique to him. Neither do I see much of myself in him – I just see Freddy. I wonder as he grows older whether I will see things that are definitely a product of his paternity. I read somewhere that the real reason children do well when raised by both their own biological parents is because they can understand both sides of themselves. Say Freddy inherits his biological dad's bad teenage skin – the originator of that gene would probably be better at dealing with it than someone with no experience of it. Then again, this is a pretty weak argument and I'm sure adopted children have no problem working through some of their biological traits and Clearasil regime themselves.

'Does he miss me?' is the question that scares the shit out of me the most. There is a risk that Freddy could feel some sort of rejection when he's older. It's important he knows that Barry's decision genuinely was all to do with himself and nothing to do with Freddy. Barry wasn't ready; he was scared; he ran away. I think the most important thing I can do is drill it into my son that the decision was NOTHING to do with him.

For now, if someone asks Freddy if he has a daddy, he just says 'NOPE!' in the same way he would if someone asked him if he has a sister. He knows he has a nanny, mummy and grandad and that's plenty in his mind. This might seem frivolous to some, but think about it – what would you prefer? In the past, I've been met with a bit of trouble (yep, Nicky Campbell, I'm looking at you again) when I've called his biological dad a 'sperm donor', but for our family, that's as much of a role as he has ever played. Biology doesn't make family. Barry biologically parented Freddy but 'fatherhood' is a totally different ball game.

Whatever you do, don't Google 'boys without fathers' because wow, will you be hit by an avalanche of shit. A true slew of horrifying scare stories that even a *Daily Mail* editor would refine for 'coming on a little strong, perhaps'. According to a quick search, children of single parents are more likely to be drug addicts, anti-social, depressed, violent – basically, anything that you wouldn't want for your child, they are more likely to be just that. For a society where one in three marriages end in divorce – meaning a LOT of us will be single parents at some time or another – this is pretty unsettling to say the least. There is only so far you can go with this destructive thinking and eventually you must draw a line under it for your own sanity. After all, I made my decision and Barry made his – and now we are living with the consequences.

So I say, ignore all that and let's look at things a little more calmly. A quarter of kids are now living in families headed by single parents like me so for the sake of the future of humanity, we should all hope those stats are misleading or that is a lot of psychopaths we have on our hands. Rather than this negativity, why don't we spread a little hope? If we look at things on a case-by-case basis then the future could be bright. There is good news that no one ever tells you about us single-parent families.

A documentary called *In a Perfect World* follows eight sons whose fathers aren't around, all from different socioeconomic backgrounds and living in America. These men each grew up to be good fathers themselves and somehow swerved all of the horrific predictions that 'empirical evidence' had for them. In fact, if anything, they grew up to be totally committed and noticeably loving parents to their children. Each of them spoke of their mothers as an inspiration – which seems to be a common thread amongst men who were brought up solely by their mum. The men also grew up to be incredibly mindful and sensitive in their relationships with women. Indeed, we do always say that by being raised by me and a troop of gay uncles, Freddy is going to make the most fabulous boyfriend one day. Somehow all the men in the film actually managed to show empathy and compassion for their AWOL dads.

These are the types of stories we should be showing our children, particularly children of single-parent families. Particularly *teenagers* of single-parent families, who are all too aware of the negative 'evidence' so regularly bandied about by the mainstream media. The film's director Daphne McWilliams says that while it would be wrong to claim that it's a positive thing to be raised without a dad, it is possible to raise a fatherless child and have no negative outcome. And that's just it, really – in a PERFECT world, Freddy would have two loving parents, of course, but there are very few things in life that are perfect.

If you're looking for them, though, there are countless examples of successful men and women who have grown up without a parent:

### Angelina Jolie

Angie's parents separated when she was just tiny, meaning she was raised mainly by her mother. Something that didn't stop her going on to star in a bajillion films and become a Hollywood A-lister.

### Paloma Faith

The singer was raised by her British mother and never had any contact with her Spanish biological Dad. Despite suffering some awful health problems, Paloma says her Mum did an 'amazing job' all on her own.

### Dizzee Rascal

After his Dad sadly died, now superstar rapper Dizzee was raised by his single Mum who he credits for encouraging his music and buying him his first ever turntables.

### Justin Bieber

After giving birth age just eighteen, Pattie Mallette, mother of pop legend Justin Bieber, brought up her son essentially on her own with his dad opting in and out of his life.

### Selena Gomez

Pop star extraordinaire Selena says she's 'extra close' to her mum after growing up with just the two of them. Her mum had her at age sixteen and she has said it was their money problems that prompted them to get her into acting.

## Ariana Grande

Grammy award-winning singer Ariana Grande was brought up by just her mum and her siblings after her parents divorced when she was eight. She calls her mum the most 'badass woman you will ever meet'.

## Leonardo DiCaprio

The parents of Oscar winner and just generally brilliant film-maker, Leo DiCaprio, divorced when he was one. Facing money problems, his mum was the one who got him into acting.

## Jared Leto

In his acceptance speech for his Oscar in 2014, Jared Leto was quick to thank his single mum who raised him to be – rather than a depressed, gambling/drug/sex addict with an anger problem – an Oscar winner.

Father absence *could* have lasting, causal effects on children's life outcomes. But at the same time, making hasty generalisations is just weak and illogical. There can be anomalies and trends can change entirely – just look at how fast Tamagotchis came and went. If we just look at oversimplified or biased statistics then we are bound to feel hopeless – but the point is that single parents like me are *not* faceless statistics. You can't let the broad strokes of statistics dictate your life. Plus, for those children of single mums who do have bad outcomes, there is generally an exacerbating factor such as secrecy, just plain bad parenting by the mother, a less than great support system, or having known and then lost the father.

It's the quality of the relationships that the child does have that affects them in the long term – not the ones they don't have. Just like I told that little boy, my son has PLENTY of super-strong relationships to own and enjoy and learn from throughout his life. Enough to ensure he can cope with the loss of one that he never knew anyway. People say children of single parents are worse off because they don't see first-hand what a good romantic relationship looks like – but all Freddy needs to do is look at his grandparents. They've been married for coming up to thirty years and are the perfect example of spouses. Well, that is when my mum's not moaning at my dad for being in the pub. But overall, Freddy sees plenty of good relationships, for example Uncles Carl and Mike, Uncles Phil and Adrien, Auntie Laura and Uncle Richard.

I totally understand if my son one day wants another perspective other than mine and that's why he's been well equipped with aunties and uncles galore that I hope he can turn to if he needs someone else to talk to. The real problem with being a single parent is TIME: we have to do two jobs with just one body. So, the risk is being overwhelmed by this and not being able to spread yourself out enough. It's not a MAN we're missing as such but, I guess, a parenting partner.

On the plus side, your kid will see how hard it is to juggle all of life's balls so I hope that this will teach mine a lesson that life can be tricky but that it is what you make it. I also hope Freddy will learn from all this that you can deal with anything life throws at you and he'll have the ability to adjust to new situations and be a wonderful, resilient adult of the future. Not one of those elusive snowflakes that Piers Morgan bangs on about on *Good Morning Britain*. I also hope I can teach Freddy that hard work pays off and independence is important – no one has to rely on anyone for anything if they don't want to. Already, our bond is so strong because we have experienced so much together and our paths into each other's lives were not exactly typical. Our uniqueness is what's bonded us so closely and I will always be so thankful for the love that we share.

There are few times it really stands out that our family isn't going to make it into a John Lewis ad anytime soon. One is when we are with a male friend and people assume they are Freddy's dad so refer to him as 'Daddy' when they talk to Freddy, much to his confusion. When he first started noticing this happening he'd only ever read about 'daddies' in books and couldn't understand what was going on. The other is the third Sunday in June – Father's Day. Some single mums say this is the day they dread the most, that it fucks them up more than Valentine's Day. But we just say that Grandad is my daddy so we address all our cards and presents to him.

So far, Freddy's never questioned anything but apparently it's all set to kick in around ages four and five. This is when children really start to question their identities and those from single-parent families are most likely to ask: 'Why don't I have two parents like everyone else?' But the idea of 'everyone else' is surely going past its sell-by date? One in four families are now single-parent families. Not to mention the increasing rates of solo IVF, gay surrogacy and blended families. Different is fast becoming the new normal. Even though I appreciate how much smaller the percentage is.

But I suppose what I'm trying to say and what I hope Freddy will realise is that every upbringing is unique. The nuclear family served us well, but this is no longer the 1950s so could we now be making way for something a little more dynamic? Something a little closer to what so many of us are actually living? Even though every family is similar in the most part, in that we all just get up in the morning and cross our fingers that we can keep ourselves and our kid alive until bedtime. We're more similar than we are different, when you break it down.

Let's not forget that if you emphasise the importance of dads specifically, then you disregard the success of same-sex female parents. And the three decades of research that points towards the children of same-sex couples growing up just as successfully and emotionally well rounded as those of mixed-sex couples. Surely 'dad' is just a label and by dropping it we can see that a child from any family set-up can succeed with the right love and support. The mere fact a man is missing from our household is about as problematic as constantly leaving the toilet seat up. Parenting over biology, please.

The main thing Freddy needs to know is that different doesn't equal wrong. I think by growing up in a nontraditional family, Freddy will be open-minded to other family set-ups that don't consist of a mummy and a daddy. And he will probably be more comfortable if any of these lies in his own future. In addition, because single parents do it all I'm hoping that my boy will have an enlightened view of gender roles and challenge traditional expectations of what a man or woman can or can't do. I shave my legs, so I'm sure I can work out how best to shave a face.

Will Freddy be just fine without a dad? Absolutely. There are far worse things life could throw at us than that. There has been a loss, there is a void – but I'm doing my best to fill that void with people who do want to be in Freddy's life. And lots and lots of love. If we've each got our fair share of loving relationships, then the rest is just semantics.

# EPILOGUE

# LET'S GET REAL –
# FINAL WORD

Now, I know what some of you are thinking: 'Yeah, you and how many other million women are single mums?' And yes, you would be right – there are a lot of us. So what makes me special? Well, nothing. And that's exactly why I am telling you my story. Because it's unremarkable in the fact it's happening to women every day all over the world. So, you would have thought that by now we'd be a little more understood and supported instead of judged. However, the fact is, NAH, we aren't and that's why I've written this book.

Recently, I read about a single-parent family who were told they couldn't buy a family cinema ticket because they 'weren't a real family'. This made me as mad as Tyra Banks when Tiffany left *America's Next Top Model*. They *are* a family. Families come in ALL shapes and sizes, and companies, policy makers and individuals need to wise up to this. The average single mum stays a single parent for FIVE YEARS. That's a long time to not even be eligible for a cut-price trip to the flicks. I hope this story speaks to the women who have experienced what I have and to let them know they're doing all right, more than all right actually. They are more than enough for their children.

Of course I can't predict the future, and I don't know how my son will feel about his situation in a few years' time, as much as I can preach that it's nothing but positive. But likewise, the presence of two parents doesn't automatically mean happiness and security either. Like ALL mums, I can just do my best and cross my fingers. What I know is that WE are a team, WE are a unit and so far, so good. I look at that beautiful kid and think, 'YEAH, I DID THAT,' and that's enough for me.

Single mums or single mums-to-be, don't fear. You got this, trust me.

# TEN LESSONS SINGLE MOTHERHOOD HAS TAUGHT ME

**P**hew! That was a lot to take in. A whole book, in fact. So for those of you who like those listicle-type things like off Buzzfeed, here are ten lessons single motherhood has taught me. A summary of sorts, just like at the end of your GCSE revision books. Only I won't make you do an exam after.

### 1. *Babies make your body do crazy things*

I never knew I could love that hard but I also never knew I'd still be lactating three years later (yep, really). Also, what a cruel twist that pregnancy makes you horny – who knew? Your body will stretch, become obsessed with KFC and then somehow it will all feel like a distant memory or some sort of weird carb-obsessed dream – probably to trick you into doing it all again.

2. *No one should go clubbing pregnant*

You won't look 'just like the woman in *Spice World*', whatever your well-intentioned, drunk mate says. Especially if you are coerced into dancing to Liberty X's 'Just a Little'. Also, I would probably advise my pregnant self to avoid Lovebox festival and stay in with my Michelle Heaton exercise DVD instead but hindsight is a fine thing.

3. *Dating isn't the be all and end all*

It took me a fair few mistakes and weird sandy encounters to realise it is possible to enjoy the relationships I had rather than focusing on the ones I was missing. Being in a romantic relationship doesn't make your life any more complete than when you aren't. Dwell on what you've GOT. And invest in a decent vibrator. My family isn't traditional, but it's also not incomplete and we don't need a dad-shaped piece to complete our puzzle.

4. *I forgive Freddy's biological dad*

When I started writing this book I can see now that I was still angry. But I've since realised that he made his decision for a reason and I've learned to respect it. He *did* do me a favour, even though it took me a while to understand it.

## 5. *Families come in all shapes and sizes*

It's the capacity to love that is what's important. Whether a family has two mummies, two daddies, or just one of either – there is no invisible ranking system. Anyone who thinks otherwise is living in the Stone Age.

## 6. *Mums come in all shapes and sizes*

There is no stereotype mum just like there is no stereo-type woman. I'm not sure why I was so terrified of other mothers – I think it was my own fear of rejection. Plus the fact I went into this knowing zero people who had a baby. Turns out, they don't bite after all. In fact, some are pretty darn awesome.

## 7. *Good friendships can survive anything*

It doesn't matter whether you veer off to opposite sides of the universe (coincidentally how it feels when one of you has a baby), a real friendship will be enough to keep you united. Yeah, your immediate existences and daily lives may have become different, but a shared love of *Heat* magazine and RuPaul can see you through anything.

## 8. *Mothers* can *do anything they want*

We aren't as free as single people to just decide what we want and go out and get it; it takes us a bit longer and it is always going to be that bit more difficult, but it's not impossible. Your abilities and talents don't disappear the minute the sperm meets that pesky egg.

9. *Life plans are there to be edited*

Life can take so many unexpected turns, you'd think we'd know to expect the unexpected by now. So if things take you by surprise, just slip and slide. You'll surprise yourself with your ability to adapt and who knows? It could turn out to be even more fabulous than what you thought you had planned anyway.

10. *Motherhood has made me happier than anything before or since*

Mel C was right – nothing compares to it. I love my life because Freddy is in it to make it sparkle every day.

And finally, that lady at Marie Stopes was right . . . a baby really does only need one person's love.

# FURTHER RESOURCES

Without this lot, life would have been much less fabulous for me. So I hope that having this list will help you a lot too . . .

## Marie Stopes

They discuss your options with no bias and total anonymity.
www.mariestopes.org.uk
0345 300 8090

## Bumpology: The Myth-busting Pregnancy Book for Curious Parents-to-be *by Linda Geddes*

This book got me through pregnancy and now I buy it for all my pregnant friends. It's so good I'd like to buy ten copies and throw them at pregnant women on the tube.

## PANDAS Foundation

In my lowest moments, I found out that pre-natal depression is as much a thing as post-natal depression. If you worried you might be suffering then these are your people.

www.pandasfoundation.org.uk

0843 28 98 401

## KFC

Tell the Colonel Amy sent you.

## Tax credits calculator

There's nothing to be ashamed of in checking what you are entitled to when you live in a world where prices are geared toward two incomes.

www.gov.uk/tax-credits-calculator

## Gingerbread

Supporting single parents since 1918. This lot have your back and are there to answer questions about all aspects of single parenthood.

www.gingerbread.org.uk

0808 802 0925

## Mush

Available in the App Store. It's kind of like Tinder, but for mums . . . in the least weird way possible. Basically, a swipey way to make mum friends.

www.letsmush.com

## Pizzup

A REAL night out for women who just happen to be mums – and last time Artful frickin' Dodger played! Now this is where I go to find like-minded mamas.

www.facebook.com/themumblingsPIZZUP/

## Babycentre

Here you can make a profile and track your pregnancy progress via fruit. Who doesn't want to know how their little grape and eventually cantaloupe melon is getting on? I also love this because you can also join a birth club correlating to your due date, full of mums ready to pop at the same time as you. Kind of like an online NCT group, I imagine.

www.babycentre.co.uk

## Mumsnet

It's not a trusted resource and on the front of Birds Eye chicken fillets for nothing. These guys know their shit when it comes to babies. Plus, sometimes it's just fun to login to read the mum rants in the forum section. There is always someone having a worse day than you on mumsnet.

www.mumsnet.com

## Bubble

This app connects you with babysitters galore for all those times you fancy a crap date or a glass of vino with your mates.

www.joinbubble.com

## Hoop

Need something to do with the bambino? This app links you with the best classes and workshops in your area.

www.hoop.co.uk

## Student Nannies

Struggling with the childcare/career struggle? Find a support network of smart, local university students who can help out after school, during school holidays and on ad hoc basis. They've got artists, actors, musicians, linguists and even a rocket scientist signed up.

www.studentnannies.com

# ACKNOWLEDGEMENTS

When I knew I wanted to write a book I remember looking on the back of my favourite one, Bryony Gordon's *The Wrong Knickers*. It said it was published by a company called Headline and I thought: 'Oh, that one would just be a pipe dream.' But here we are, and I still can't believe it.

Jenny Stallard, let's be honest – this was all your idea. At risk of a *Social Network*-esque lawsuit – remember when I suggested some rubbish Mother's Day ideas and you said, 'Why don't you write about YOU?' Well, you kicked this whole thing off really! Thank you for commissioning 'Dating Confessions of a Single Mum' – without that I don't think I'd be writing this now.

To Tracey Blake, my editor at *Metro* – who else would have let me interview all my ex-boyfriends in a national newspaper? You once tweeted 'someone give this girl a book deal!' – would you believe they actually did?! Working with you was always a dream.

Lauren Gardner, my fabulous agent, who planted the seed for a book however many moons ago – you are the best and most beautiful to work with and we must always wear our matching bobble hats for good luck.

Thanks to everyone at Headline. Grace Paul, the best editor. I knew from the moment we met during that meeting with Georgina that you just 'got it' and were the only person to hold my hand in making this the best it could be. I trust your judgement implicitly. Jessica Farrugia, you are a blaze of beauty, and your enthusiasm for this book has been like fuel to me during the writing process. Helena Fouracre, you had me at our mutual love of *Angus, Thongs and Full-Frontal Snogging* – thank you for everything.

My mum for spending (literally) hours reading through every single chapter with me. You are the kindest person I know or will ever know. You are also super-funny – which made you the perfect first draft editor. My dad, for being the best grandad ever and worth 979,435 dads. I hope I've made Grandad Bill proud. My brother Martin, you will never read this, but your absolute belief in me will drive me always.

*This Morning*, *Judge Rinder*, that thing Ben Shephard does with the slot machines – you may have been on mute but you were there for me throughout the writing process.

I'd like to thank Julia White (then Yahoo now Twitter), for giving me a chance with every idea, however crap, and for believing in me and getting me to my dream destination – telly via *Good Morning Britain*! While on the subject, I'd like to thank Piers Morgan for telling me to shut up – no Piers, I can't and I won't – here's over 70,000 more of my words just for you.

To every editor who saw that families do come in all shapes

and sizes and commissioned me to write as much – Radhika at BBC3, Steve at the *Guardian*, Hannah at *Fabulous*, Leanne at *Glamour*, Carren, Ali and Dawn at *Good Morning Britain*, Lucy at Babycentre, Kira at *Woman*, Jane Garvey, everyone at 5Live. To everyone who has ever put me in front of a camera; everyone at BigDog, especially Bethan and Joe; and my agents at BMA.

For Oliver for telling me when I wasn't funny and repeatedly telling me to 'be more bold'. Thank you, darling. I hope it was bold enough for you in the end.

To Caitlin Moran for telling me to put my manuscript in a drawer for four weeks and come back to it with fresh eyes. If you find even one line of this faintly amusing then all my dreams will have come true.

Godfather Lorcan, all my friends who put up with me even at my most, as Carl would say, 'self-indulgent'(!).

And of course, my Freddy. You are my superstar, my favourite person in the whole world. You make everything sparkle and I love you.

I could go on but modesty – and remembering Gwyneth at the Oscars – inclines me to stop here.